BRITAIN IN OLD PHOTOGRAPHS

DUDLEY

HILARY ATKINS
DIANE MATTHEWS
SAMANTHA ROBINS

SUTTON PUBLISHING LIMITED

Sutton Publishing Limited
Phoenix Mill · Thrupp · Stroud
Gloucestershire · GL5 2BU

First published 1998

Copyright © Hilary Atkins, Diane Matthews,
Samantha Robins, 1998

Title page photograph: Castle Hill at its junction
with Trindle Road, showing the drinking
fountain and the Station Hotel, *c.* 1900.
Front cover: Elephants at Dudley Castle, 1950.
Back cover: Tower Street, Dudley, *c.* 1900.

British Library Cataloguing in Publication Data
A catalogue record for this book is available from the
British Library.

ISBN 0-7509-1961-2

Typeset in 10/12 Perpetua.
Typesetting and origination by
Sutton Publishing Limited.
Printed in Great Britain by
Ebenezer Baylis, Worcester.

The photographs included here are a selection from some 16,000 held by Dudley Archives and Local History Service based at Mount Pleasant Street, Coseley, covering the whole area of the present Metropolitan Borough. The Service is always interested to hear about other local photographs which people may be willing to donate or lend for copying.

THE BLACK COUNTRY SOCIETY

This voluntary society, affiliated to the Civic Trust, was founded in 1967 as a reaction to the trend of the late 1950s and early 1960s to amalgamate everything into large units and in the Midlands to sweep away the area's industrial heritage in the process.

The general aim of the Society is to create interest in the past, present and future of the Black Country, and early on it campaigned for the establishment of an industrial museum. In 1975 the Black Country Museum was started by Dudley Borough Council on 26 acres of totally derelict land adjoining the grounds of Dudley Castle. This has developed into an award-winning museum which attracts over 250,000 visitors annually.

At the Black Country Museum there is a boat dock fully equipped to restore narrow boats of wood and iron and different boats can be seen on the dock throughout the year. From behind the Bottle and Glass Inn visitors can travel on a canal boat into Dudley Canal Tunnel, a memorable journey to see spectacular limestone caverns and the fascinating Castle Mill Basin.

There are over two thousand members of the Black Country Society and all receive the quarterly magazine *The Blackcountryman*, of which over 119 issues have been published since its founding in 1967. In the whole collection there are some 1,700 authoritative articles on all aspects of the Black Country by historians, teachers, researchers, students, subject experts and ordinary folk with an extraordinary story to tell. The whole constitutes a unique resource about the area and is a mine of information for students and researchers who frequently refer to it. Many schools and libraries are subscribers. Three thousand copies of the magazine are printed each quarter. It is non-commercial, and contributors do not receive payment for their articles.

PO Box 71 · Kingswinford · West Midlands DY6 9YN

CONTENTS

Introduction   5

1.   Castle, Zoo & Priory   7

2.   Churches & Chapels   19

3.   Municipal Life   31

4.   Housing   41

5.   Education   51

6.   Transport   63

7.   Industry   73

8.   Shops & Services   83

9.   Public Houses & Cinemas   93

10. Leisure   103

11. A Change of Scene   115

     Acknowledgements   126

The fountain, Dudley Market Place, *c.* 1900. The fountain was designed by James Forsythe and given by the Earl of Dudley. It replaced the Old Town Hall which stood on the site and was demolished in 1860. It was unveiled by the Earl and Countess of Dudley on 17 October 1867.

INTRODUCTION

Dudley, including Netherton, was historically an island of Worcestershire surrounded by Staffordshire (although Dudley Castle was in fact in Staffordshire until 1928), and is often considered to be the capital of the Black Country. Dudley was a settlement in early times and the name is probably of Saxon origins, from Dudda's Leah, Dudda's clearing. The castle was in existence by the time of the Domesday Survey of 1086 which records that 'William Fitz Ansculf holds Dudley and there is his castle'. It was a natural site for a castle dominating the surrounding area.

The town grew up around the castle and to the south of it, consisting in medieval times of one long street, the present High Street between the two churches of St Thomas's and St Edmund's. Both churches existed as early as the twelfth century, and it is surprising that a small town should have the two. It is generally considered that St Thomas's served the town and St Edmund's the castle and its lords. There was also the Cluniac priory of St James, founded by Gervase Paganel between 1160 and 1180 as a cell or daughter house of Much Wenlock Priory, Shropshire.

Dudley continued as a small market town influenced by only a few outside events until the nineteenth century. These events included a visit of Elizabeth I to the castle in 1575, the inspection of the castle as a possible place of imprisonment for Mary, Queen of Scots in 1585 and the siege of the castle during the Civil War in 1646.

The rich mineral resources of the area have been exploited since medieval times. Dudley sat on the rich Ten Yard coal seam which is said to define the Black Country, and also benefited from deposits of clay, ironstone and limestone. It was the Industrial Revolution, and the improvements in mining techniques and transport it brought, which created an explosion in the extraction of these natural resources. This in turn led to the development of metal manufacturing industries for which the area was well known, such as iron foundries, chain and anchor making, and anvil and vice making.

As Dudley had no navigable rivers, transportation until the late eighteenth century had to be by roads, which were often in bad repair when the parish had responsibility for them, making travel slow. The situation improved under the turnpike trusts but tolls made journeys expensive. The canal came to Dudley in the 1780s, allowing larger quantities of goods to be transported more quickly and cheaply. The canals in their turn were superseded by the railway from 1850. Dudley had two stations, one in the town and another at Blowers Green, until the lines were closed following the Beeching Report in 1963.

The growth of industry spurred on by ever-expanding markets led to an influx of people coming to work in the town's mines and factories. Between 1801 and 1851 the population of Dudley increased from about 10,000 to more than 37,000. This sudden sharp rise resulted in badly built and unplanned houses springing up in the courts and yards of older town houses. These became the town's slums and suffered from poor lighting, lack of ventilation, dampness, overcrowding and an appalling lack of sanitation. Despite numerous public health reports during the nineteenth and early twentieth centuries, and enabling Acts of Parliament, Dudley Council did not act to improve working class housing in the town until 1912, when a sub-committee was established to look into the problem. The first council houses were built in 1919 at Brewery Fields, but the clearance of the slums did not really get under way until 1930. The programme then continued well after the war. Initially, the borough faced a big problem in finding suitable land on which to build. In 1926 the Priory Estate was purchased from the Earl of Dudley with the intention of building there. However, part of it lay outside the borough boundary and was, therefore, not available to the Corporation. This was overcome with an extension of the boundaries, granted in 1928. Work then began on the Priory housing estate, which was used to rehouse people from the town centre slums.

The growth of population also brought the need for new churches and the creation of new ecclesiastical parishes, especially in the 1840s. The town was administered by the manorial courts until the establishment of the Town or Improvement Commissioners under a local Act of Parliament in 1791 'for the better paving, cleansing, lighting, watching and other ways of improving the Town'. The provisions of the Public Health Act of 1848 were adopted in 1852 with the appointment of the Local Board of Health. This followed the report of housing conditions by William Lee for the General Board of Health in 1851.

Dudley gained borough status in 1865, on obtaining a charter of incorporation. It became a county borough council after the Local Government Act of 1888. There were extensions to the borough in 1928 and 1953 and again in 1966 following the West Midlands Order of 1965. Dudley became a metropolitan borough under the 1974 local government reorganisation.

Dudley has continued to change and develop in more recent years. The town centre has suffered, perhaps more than most, from the rise in out-of-town shopping, and many of the large multiple stores have withdrawn. The decline in heavy industry has also been marked. However, Dudley continues to develop, with new housing being built on previously disused industrial sites, a new bypass to the south of the town, and plans to develop the Castle Gates area, off Birmingham Road, as a leisure facility, and bring the railway back to Dudley. Through all of this, the castle has remained the dominant feature of the town – rarely out of view, as a reminder of Dudley's long history.

CHAPTER ONE

CASTLE, ZOO & PRIORY

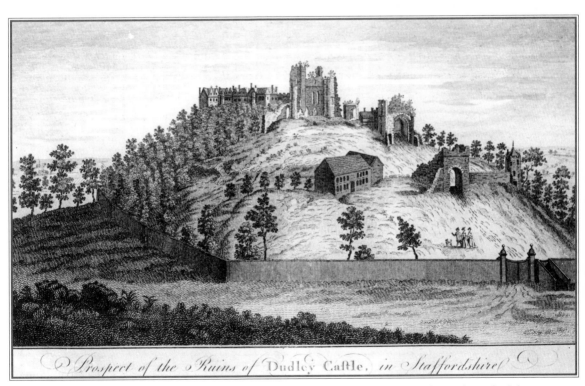

*An eighteenth-century engraving of Dudley Castle ruins. Legend has it that a wooden castle was built here
in about 700 by a Saxon lord called Dud or Dado, and Dudley is one of the few castles mentioned in
Domesday Book. It was the historical seat of the barons of Dudley, but had suffered a long period of neglect
before being seen as a romantic ruin by artists and antiquarians in the late eighteenth century.*

The castle gates in Castle Hill at the turn of the century, presumably at around Whitsun, since a poster advertising the Castle Fetes, along with balloon ascents and a display by the Royal Marine artillery, can be clearly seen attached to the gatepost. The statue is of the first Earl of Dudley and was erected in 1888. It now faces in the other direction, having been turned in the 1930s to even out the wear. The building just inside the gates on the left is now The Fellows pub, and busy traffic lights stand outside, while the cottages on the right are seemingly unchanged.

Opposite top. A large crowd gathered to watch a military review, 1860s. The soldiers taking part can be seen in the extreme foreground. The castle had not been a permanent home nor a tenable fortress since the Civil War when Dudley was a royalist stronghold. After its garrison surrendered on the King's orders in 1646, the castle was sleighted and never, thereafter, refortified. Part of it was occupied later, although the Ward family had moved to Himley Hall. The living quarters were destroyed by fire in 1750.

Opposite bottom. Two Victorian ladies in the castle courtyard, showing the view from the chapel to the northern gateway. The Ward family had long since ceased to live at the castle, but they owned it until the 1930s and allowed the townspeople access. William Ward, the 3rd Viscount Dudley, had the castle grounds beautified, heaps of limestone removed from the keep and one of the towers raised in the late eighteenth century. The grounds were open to the public for recreation, free of charge, until the zoo opened in 1937.

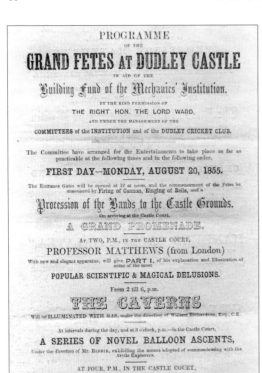

The first page of the programme for the 1855 Castle Fete. Fetes were held in the castle courtyard from 1850 through to the First World War. The entertainment lasted for three days over the Whitsun holiday and the proceeds were used to benefit local charities, such as the Mechanics Institute and Guest Hospital.

A scene (below) from the Castle Fetes in Edwardian times. The grounds are clearly busy and everyone seems to be in their 'Sunday Best'. On the right a bandstand has been set up and a concert seems to be in progress, while on the left a hot air balloon is being inflated and causing some interest in the crowd. Balloon ascents were always a popular feature of the fetes.

Wellington Road Methodist Church, c. 1970. The Wellington Road Primitive Methodist Church was built in 1861. It ceased to be a Methodist church in 1966 following the merger of the Dudley churches, worship being held at the Wolverhampton Street church until its demolition and in temporary places until the opening of the new church in 1978. It has been used as a Sikh temple since 1970.

Priory Methodist Church on the corner of Limepit Lane and Laurel Road, Priory Estate, 1965. The church was opened in 1938 to serve the new Priory Estate. By 1979 it was being shared with the First United Pentecostal Church. Services ceased to be held there in 1979 and the building was sold to the First United Church of Jesus Christ of Apostolic in 1980.

Providence Methodist Church (Methodist New Connexion), Northfield Road, Darby Hand, 1962. The church opened in 1837 and closed in 1974. It was removed from the site in 1975 and re-erected at the Black Country Living Museum by 1978.

Miss Jack's Bible Class, Netherton, 1909. Miss Jack is possibly in the front centre of this group of unnamed ladies. It has not been possible to establish exactly the place of worship with which this class was associated, but it could well have been Providence Methodist Church, Darby Hand, as the minister there from 1904 to 1909 was the Revd David Jack.

The Presbyterian Church, Wolverhampton
Street, from *Dudley: Illustrated by Photographs*,
W.H. Laxton, 1868. The foundation stone was
laid in January 1847 and the church opened in
November of the same year. It was destroyed
by fire on 25 June 1944, leaving only a roofless
shell. On 28 September 1948 the first sod was
cut on a site at the rear of the demolished
church for a new church hall, to be used until a
replacement church could be built. The
present church is in Trinity Road.

Messiah Baptist Church, Cinderbank, Netherton, 1963. This was one of the oldest Baptist churches in the
area. The church closed and was demolished in 1979, having become unsafe. Part of the burial ground
with a war memorial still remains, a reminder of where the church stood. This church (the third one) was
built in 1871. Its origins can be traced back to 1654, the date of the first entry in the 'Church Book', and
it became autonomous in 1665. The exact site of the first church is unknown, but a church was built on
this site in about 1746.

Entrance to the Old Meeting House (Unitarian Chapel), Wolverhampton Street, 1959. The first chapel was erected in 1702, destroyed by rioters in 1715 and rebuilt in 1717. Its registers date back to 1743. In 1869 the church was re-opened following restoration work. The church is now surrounded by other buildings but it is still visible through the archway, and the rear and the schoolroom can be seen from Horseley Gardens. The burial ground in the Inhedge was cleared in 1973 in connection with the development of the courts and is now part of their gardens.

King Street Congregational Church, 1955. The first chapel was built nearer New Mill Street in 1788. It became too small and a new church was built. The foundation stone was laid in 1839 and the church opened in 1840: 'Erected 1840' was inscribed above the entrance. The church joined with the Presbyterian church in Trinity Road in 1972 to become the United Reformed Church. It was closed and later demolished in the 1980s; the site was to have been redeveloped but this has not taken place and it is now derelict. The burial ground remains, although overgrown.

The Roman Catholic Church, Bourne Street, looking from Claughton Road towards Trindle Road, *c.* 1928. The church, dedicated to Our Lady and St Thomas of Canterbury, was designed by the famous Pugin and consecrated in 1842. Before this, the congregation had, from 1833, used a warehouse in Chapel Street for the celebration of Mass and in 1835 moved to a Methodist chapel.

Salvation Army Citadel, King Street, 1958. The building was sold to Woolworths in 1974 for expansion of the store, and a new citadel was erected on the site of Christ Church Congregational Church in North Street. The Army was established in Dudley by 1877, when the first meeting was held in the Temperance Hall, High Street. In 1878 they moved to a chapel in Chapel Street, then an old wooden theatre in New Hall Street and by 1885 they were at the Barracks. By 1912 they had become established in King Street.

St Thomas's Church Choir, c. 1916. The vicar, the Revd A. Gray-Maitland (vicar 1892–1917) is in the centre, J.M. (McDougal) Tait is on the right, and Fred R. McDowell is on the left – both with churchwardens' staves of office. They were churchwardens from 1915 to 1919. Ernest Davies is in the fourth row back at the left end, wearing glasses; Mr North, back row left end, was organist until his retirement in 1919; Harry Preedy is in the second row from the back, third from the right, wearing glasses; and A.H. Cutler is in the back row at the right-hand end: he was organist and choirmaster for forty years from 1919.

This is apparently a Methodist group, with Oakham House in the background, c. 1895. It has not been possible to establish so far from which church the group came, or indeed the occasion. The photographer was H. Bowler, 5 Castle Street.

CHAPTER THREE

MUNICIPAL LIFE

Old Town Hall, Market Place, from Dudley: Illustrated by Photographs, *W.H. Laxton, 1868. This building was constructed by Thomas Caddick between 1653 and 1654, and demolished in about 1860 as part of the opening up of the Market Place already begun by the demolition of Middle Row between 1835 and 1851. Towards the end of its life it had been used as a police station, lock-up and magistrates' court. The fountain given by the Earl of Dudley in 1867 was built on the site.*

Postcard view of the old police station, Priory Street, *c.* 1900. The police station and lock-up with its castellations was considered to be out of keeping with the new Town Hall and Council House, and it was intended to demolish the building after the new police station on the corner of Tower Street and New Street opened in 1941. The war intervened and the building still exists as part of the council offices. The pillars at the entrance were taken to Netherton Park but later removed, and their present whereabouts are unknown.

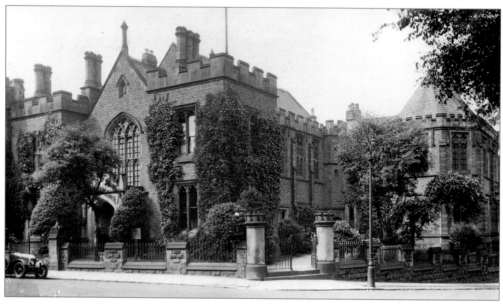

The Old Town Hall, Priory Street, possibly 1920s. This was erected by the Earl of Dudley in 1858 to replace the Old Town Hall in the Market Place, and demolished in 1933 to make way for the present Council House.

Crowds gathering to witness the arrival of the Prime Minister, the Rt. Hon. Stanley Baldwin, to open the Town Hall and War Memorial Tower (memorial to those who died in the First World War), Tuesday 16 October 1928.

The Brooke Robinson Museum, the courts and other council buildings on the corner of Priory Street and St James's Road, *c.* 1970. The Coroner's Court is still in the Town Hall: Quarter Sessions and Magistrates' Courts were held there until 1972 and 1971 respectively, Quarter Sessions being replaced by the Crown Court (held there until 1990) and now council offices. The Brooke Robinson Museum, endowed by Mr Brooke Robinson (1836–1911), opened in 1931. It was closed in the mid-1960s and the exhibits transferred to Dudley Art Gallery in 1981.

The Council House, Priory Road, viewed from the Coronation or Civic Gardens, *c.* 1970. The Council House, erected by John Dallow of Blackheath and designed by Messrs Harvey & Wicks, architects of Birmingham, was opened by the Duke of Kent on 2 December 1935. The layout of Coronation Gardens was completed in 1939 and the statue of Apollo, the gift of Mr E.J. Thompson, was unveiled by Lord Cobham in May 1939.

Free Library, School of Art and Art Gallery at the corner of St James's Road and Priory Street, *c.* 1890. The building was opened in 1884, and the Free Library moved to its present building on the other side of St James's Road in 1909. The School of Art transferred to the Technical College in 1966, the Art Gallery then occupying the whole building. The ornamental turret on the corner was removed for safety reasons in 1953. The set of meteorological instruments donated by James Smellie to commemorate his wife, mayoress in 1926, was unveiled in October 1927.

The Central Library, St James's Road, *c.* 1910, soon after its erection and opening in 1909. The building was extended and refurbished in 1966. The figures over the main entrance are by George H. Wenyon of Dudley: the one on the top is said to represent Philosophy and the ones over the entrance Science and Literature.

Netherton Library and Arts Centre, Halesowen Road, 1969. After the opening of Dudley Library in 1884 branch libraries were established at Netherton and Woodside, firstly in hired premises in 1884 (in the Market Place, Netherton). A site for a permanent library was given by the Earl of Dudley and opened as a public hall and library by the Earl and Countess of Dudley in 1894. The building was refurbished and opened as a library and arts centre in 1947.

Exterior of Woodside Library, Stourbridge Road, 1960, showing Mrs M. Dixon, Branch Supervisor, Mr Clark, caretaker, and the 1934 Rover 10 that belonged to Mr F. Regan, Deputy Borough Librarian. Woodside Branch Library was opened in rented premises in 1885, and opened in a permanent building by the Earl and Countess of Dudley in 1894 – on the same day as Netherton Branch Library; the site was also given by the Earl of Dudley.

Exterior of Dudley Wood Branch Library, Bush Road, 1961. A library service point was opened at Dudley Wood Infants' School in 1934 and a branch library at Bowling Green Junior School in 1954. This purpose-built library, designed by the Borough Architect, J.T. Lewis, was opened in July 1960.

Dudley Dispensary, on the corner of Priory and Ednam Roads, from Dudley: Illustrated by Photographs, W.H. Laxton, 1868. The Dudley Dispensary was established in 1845 as a medical charity for the relief of the sick poor. In 1861 Joseph Guest gave £1,000 and the Earl of Dudley the site, and the building opened in 1862. It continued as the Dispensary probably until the establishment of the National Health Service in 1948. The building was purchased by the Council in 1953, renovated in 1957 and used as offices. It was demolished in 1976 to make way for extensions to council offices.

Offices of the Dudley Board of Guardians (or the Poor Law Union) at the corner of St James's Road and Parsons Street, c. 1900 (pre-dating the building of the Central Library, which opened in 1909). The offices, which were opened in 1888 (they had previously been at the Town Hall, Priory Street), also included the Registrar's Office. They housed the Dudley Public Assistance Department from 1930 (the successors of the Board of Guardians) and later the Housing Department, and are still in use as council offices.

The Worcestershire Constabulary, Netherton Section, apparently outside Netherton Cricket Club, Highfield Road, 1908. The police were established in Dudley in 1840 and were part of the Worcestershire Constabulary until the establishment of the Dudley Force in 1920. The story goes that after the Boer War Dudley police were allowed to wear the bushranger type of hat.

Dudley Police Force, photographed after 1927 by Sergeant (later Inspector) A.E. (Fred) Griffiths (father of Mrs L. Price, owner of the original photograph), presumably outside the old police station, Priory Street, probably in the courtyard. The motorcycle FD 3892 was a BSA, registered to the County Borough of Dudley on 4 July 1927.

Dudley Fire Brigade's steam fire engine, *c.* 1900. The Shand Mason engine was purchased in 1899. This replaced the first engine purchased in 1871. The Chief Superintendent, Mr Speke, the captain and the engine partially manned are shown. Dudley Brigade was first established in 1834; from 1839 to 1870 cover was provided by insurance brigades. In 1871 it became the Dudley Police Fire Brigade, with the police providing the personnel. From 1941 to 1948 the brigade was part of the war-time National Fire Service, and from 1948 the Dudley Fire Brigade.

The old fire station, Priory Street, 1959, before conversion to a shop for Paynes Ltd, boot and shoe repairers, who were displaced from premises in Wolverhampton Street because of the Horseley House redevelopment. This photograph shows the original doors before conversion. The building, now a café, was opened as a fire station in 1892 on the site of the Old Glasshouse (demolished in 1886). The new fire station in Tower Street was opened in 1941.

The 65-ft Simon Snorkel Firefighting and Rescue Unit at Dudley Fire Station, after 1962. Simon Engineering of Dudley developed the snorkel for fire-fighters in 1961; it was demonstrated at Dudley Fire Station in September 1961 and later exported and used by fire brigades all over the world, the firm winning a safety award in 1965. The vehicle, 5289 FD, a Bedford 7.5-ton lorry, was registered to Simon Engineering in January 1962. Simon Engineering closed its factory in Dudley in 1994 and production was moved to Gloucester.

Dudley County Borough Fire Brigade's latest appliance outside Dudley Fire Station in Tower Street, 1967. Included in the photograph may possibly be Chief Fire and Ambulance Officer F. Wade, 1948–68 (when he retired), and T.D. Dutton, Deputy Officer from 1954.

CHAPTER FOUR

HOUSING

Alexandra Place, Bluebell Park, probably c. 1910–15. Alexandra Place was built after 1901 but before 1911, when it was first mentioned by name in a rate book. As rate book entries from 1904 show six properties listed under Old Park with exactly the same rateable value and rates payable as 1–6 Alexandra Place, it seems likely they are the same houses. Originally in Coseley parish, these properties (built by the Earl of Dudley) formed part of the Priory Estate, which was sold to Dudley Council in 1926. Dudley Council took over responsibility for these cottages at this time.

108 Blackbrook Road, Woodside, *c.* 1928. Woodside was originally separate from Dudley town, but merged with Dudley as development occurred along Stourbridge Road. The area was mainly populated by those involved in the mining and iron industries. The last entry in the electoral roll for this house was in 1930/1, when it was occupied by Cyril and Mary Bimson and also by Isaac and Thomas Lilley. It is probable that the house was demolished around this time as the council had issued a number of compulsory purchase orders for dilapidated or dangerous houses in the Woodside area.

Cawney Bank House, Oakham Road, 1961. This house was a listed building built in the late eighteenth or early nineteenth century. Local legend claims that Cromwell's troops stayed at this site before their attack on Dudley Castle in 1644. J.H. Price gave the house to the Guest Hospital in 1941 for use as a convalescent home; however, during the war the house was requisitioned by the National Fire Service. In 1948 the NHS took over the property but it was surplus to requirements and was demolished in about 1961, to make way for a new housing estate.

This long view of Court 2 Birmingham Street, *c.* 1930, shows the closeness and bad arrangement of the houses and narrowness of the passages. The houses were damp and dirty with poor ventilation, while the courts and yards were unpaved with no drainage. Following the 1930 Housing Act the Government gave subsidies to encourage local authorities to undertake extensive slum clearance. Dudley responded, and this property was part of the Birmingham Street Slum Clearance Scheme of 1930. Under this scheme an area of 34 acres was to be demolished, including 172 houses, 10 factories, 13 shops and 8 lodging houses.

A general view of the yard at 6–12 Guests Fold, *c.* 1930. Guests Fold was a 10 ft wide alleyway with houses on both sides. This too was part of the Birmingham Street Slum Clearance area, together with Birmingham Street, Fisher Street and Portersfield. Compulsory purchase orders were issued and demolition started in 1932; by 1933 only three properties remained. A total of 819 people needed to be rehoused: 592 of these people were having to share thirty-three communal taps. The inhabitants were rehoused mainly on the Priory Estate or Wolverton Road, the site of wooden huts built to house the munitions workers at the National Projectile Factory.

Priory Estate, proposed shopping centre, c. 1928. On 18 October 1926 Dudley Council purchased 522 acres of land at Priory Estate for £75,000 from the Earl of Dudley, where they proposed to build 3,000 houses to house a growing population and those dispossessed by slum clearance. E. Prentice Mawson, a professional town planning consultant, was asked to provide a report on developing the area. Over a third of this land was outside the borough, so in 1928 the council asked parliament for permission to extend its boundaries. This was granted only in respect of Priory Estate.

Priory Park and Estate, 1936. The 16-acre Priory Park was opened on 27 July 1932. It included sports facilities, playing areas and a sunken Italian garden. The foundation stones of the first two houses were laid on 16 July 1929. By 1939, 2,229 of the 3,694 municipal houses erected in Dudley were on the Priory Estate. Priory Road was constructed during 1932 to make a through road from the town to the New Birmingham Road. Paganel and Gervase Drives were also constructed at this time, and 100 building plots were sold to Dudley's private housebuilders.

Firing of the hutments by the Mayor, Alderman J.H. Molyneux, 19 October 1933. Nine hostels and 345 houses were built at Brewery Fields in 1916 as a temporary measure to house munitions workers. Living conditions were primitive and insanitary and slum conditions developed. Following a serious fire on 23 December 1917 (during which two blocks of houses were destroyed and seventy people made homeless) an estate fire brigade was set up. Dudley Town Council acquired the site in 1930, in order to demolish the properties and use the land for building permanent houses.

Firing of the old wooden hutments, 19 October 1933. During 1932–3 the tenants were gradually transferred to new accommodation, and on Thursday 28 September the fire brigade destroyed four hutments in a dress rehearsal for the symbolic firing of the hutments by the mayor, which destroyed 100 further hutments. The remainder were burned as they became vacant, and by 8 December 1933 the site was clear. The fire brigade had attended the site on eight occasions and the council, being appreciative of their assistance, voted to give the Chief Constable £10 to distribute to the men concerned.

A and B Ernest Road, Dudley. Dudley was the first municipal authority to erect experimental iron houses and these two, known as Mirema and Iron House, were built between 1925 and 1927 (curiously they were not allocated street numbers). Designed and constructed by the Eclipse Foundry Co., their outer walls were of cast-iron plate and the interior walls were of asbestos sheeting, with wool packed into the cavity. Only two pairs of the semi-detached houses were ever built in Dudley, and in 1989 they were dismantled and transferred to the Black Country Museum where one pair was rebuilt in 1995. (Picture reproduced by permission of the *Wolverhampton Express & Star*.)

Warrens Hall Road Flats, Sledmere Estate, *c*. 1955; they were photographed for the Dudley *Official Guide* of 1956. After the Second World War Dudley Council stated that housing was to be a priority, and in 1946 they purchased 134 acres of land on the Sledmere and Warrens Hall Estates for redevelopment. By 1954 the site at Sledmere had been levelled for house building and 507 municipal properties had been built by the end of 1956; a further 64 were expected to be finished within six months. The council announced that further developments would take place there in the future.

Barber's shop, Salop Street, Eve Hill, Dudley, 1963. Following a public enquiry in July 1962, it was confirmed that 192 sub standard properties in the Eve Hill area were to be demolished and the land redeveloped. About 5 acres of Eve Hill had been subject to compulsory purchase orders, but there was much resistance to this, one objector claiming that old people would be unable to 'enjoy their pigeons and their dogs' or afford the rent of new properties. By 1967 the flats were being built on the site, three tower blocks being completed by 1970.

View from the rear common yard of 1–4 Hill Street, Netherton, and 64–71 Simms Lane, early 1960s. These houses were demolished in about 1965–6 under the Dudley Corporation Simms Lane No. 1 CPO 1963, as the Medical Officer of Health condemned them as unfit for human habitation. The council planned to redevelop the site, and their proposals included the building of five blocks of four-storey flats, thirty-four terraced houses and eighty-nine garages, so that people being rehoused would not have to move away from the area they had lived in all their lives, thus retaining the community spirit.

10–17 Inhedge, front elevation, c. 1960. These houses between the burial ground and Cross Street were demolished after the town council acquired them following the Dudley Corporation Old Dock (Dudley) CPO. Objections to the compulsory purchase of no. 15 (together with nos 23, 24 and 25) were received, but the council stated they were 'required for a proposed inner ring road, the remainder for a car park'.

Frontal view of 14–21 Great Hill, Dudley. No details have been found relating to the demolition of these houses, but 1–5 Great Hill were demolished in the early 1960s as part of the slum clearance programme of the Old Dock area. Electoral rolls reveal inhabitants for 14–21 Great Hill in October 1954, but by October 1955 only occupiers for nos 15 and 21 were listed and by October 1956 they too had disappeared. It is not certain whether the houses were demolished then or later with the remainder of the street.

The Old Dock area before the 1963 redevelopment, showing the narrow, badly aligned streets. A public enquiry in June 1960 about the three compulsory purchase orders served in this area heard that there were 470 unfit properties and 594 families to be rehoused. Most houses were damp, overcrowded and in poor repair, with shared lavatories and water supply in a communal back yard. Accommodation for 600 families was planned by providing flats nearby, thus maintaining the same population density. The displaced businesses were to be offered accommodation in Flood Street or Harts Hill. The acquisition of these sites was expected to cost £268,500.

Queens Cross Flats, Dudley, 1968. The first multi-storey flats to be built in Dudley were to rehouse people from the Old and New Dock slum clearance areas. Four blocks, each containing eighty-seven flats, were constructed at a cost of just over £1 million by George Wimpey & Co. Ltd. Wychbury Court was completed first and officially opened in November 1964 by the mayor, Councillor W.G.K. Griffiths. The flats were named Clent Court, Claverley Court, Romsley Court and Wychbury Court after the areas which could be seen from them. All four blocks were completed by June 1965, and occupied by July.

Russells Hall Estate from Himley Road, during the opening of the 10,000th municipal house in the borough, 1963. This photograph is reproduced by kind permission of the *Wolverhampton Express & Star*. Dudley Council purchased the derelict 250-acre site in 1947, levelling it in 1952 and moving over 3,000,000 cu. ft of earth. The land was allowed to settle for five years before building work commenced in 1957, and the houses were built on reinforced concrete rafts to ensure greater stability. Over 2,000 houses and seven schools were to be built over ten years. The first house was completed and let in March 1958.

CHAPTER FIVE

EDUCATION

Holly Hall Schools, Stourbridge Road, from Dudley: Illustrated by Photographs, W.H. Laxton, 1868.
*The Schools in Woodside facing Stourbridge Road were erected in 1860–1 through the generosity of A.B.
Cochrane of Woodside Ironworks and opened on 3 June 1861. They were used for church services from 1868
until the opening of St Augustine's in 1884. The school, later Woodside Middle School, was closed in 1983
following its amalgamation with Holly Hall First School to become Highgate Primary. Some of the buildings
on the site became a day centre and others were demolished in about 1987, including the frontage.*

St Edmund's Schools, Birmingham Street, from Blocksidge's *Dudley Almanack,* 1901. The foundation stone was laid in 1848, the site being given by Lord Ward. The school closed in 1974, moving to a site in Beechwood Road and amalgamating with St John's School, later becoming the C. of E. Primary School of St Edmund and St John. The building is now a mosque, which opened in 1978.

St Thomas's Old School, King Street, 1957. The foundation stone of the school was laid on 25 March 1847. In 1936 the school moved to new premises alongside, following the road widening. It amalgamated with Jessons Schools and Park Primary School in 1970 and moved from the site. The old buildings were taken over by Hill & Co. (Dudley), cloth manufacturers, later trading as Pathfinder, menswear store, which closed in 1993.

Blue Coat School, Dixons Green (Bean Road), *c.* 1900. The school was established in 1706/7, and was, in the early years, in different locations. In 1812 a new school was built in Fisher Street which was shared with the Female School of Industry. This building was erected in 1869. The school moved to Beechwood Road in 1970 on the closure of Rosland County Secondary School, and the Bean Road premises were used as an annexe until 1981. The school amalgamated with Dudley Grammar School and Dudley Girls High School to become Castle High School in 1989.

Stafford Street Schools at the junction of Stafford and Steppingstone Streets, 1959. An 'infantile school' was established on approximately this site in 1821 and was enlarged in 1894. It was closed in 1961 and was later used as the motor taxation office and also as a temporary library during the refurbishment of the central library in 1966. It was also used as the magistrates' courts from 1971 until the opening of the new courts in the Inhedge in 1976. It was later demolished and a day centre now occupies the site.

Old Holly Hall Secondary School, Stourbridge Road, 1966. This was formerly Harts Hill Board School. The Harts Hill Boys' & Girls' Board School opened in 1875. It later became Harts Hill Mixed School and a Secondary School from 1927, and Holly Hall County Secondary School from 1943. It was replaced by Holly Hall Secondary School, Scotts Green, in 1966. Part of the site is now used as a training centre and part by the Scouts.

The exterior of Holly Hall Secondary School, Scotts Green, photographed for the Dudley County Borough Official Guide, 1968. The school was opened in 1966 to replace the school in Stourbridge Road, and is now Holly Hall Grant-Maintained School.

Halesowen Road Schools, at the junction of Halesowen Road and Saltwells Road (known as the 'Iron Schools'), 1959. The schools opened on 14 March 1885, were closed in 1962 and replaced by the new Saltwells Secondary School. They were demolished in 1963. These were temporary buildings when erected in 1884 and were only guaranteed to stand for seven years, because of the risk of subsidence caused by mining.

The Main Hall at Halesowen Road Schools, showing the construction, 1959. They were constructed with a frame of iron girders clad with corrugated sheets and so were known as the 'Iron Schools'. The heating pipes, dais and classrooms opening off should be noted. The schools were also known locally as 'the Watercress College' because of their proximity to the watercress beds near Worcester Road.

Wolverhampton Street Schools prior to demolition, probably *c*. 1965. The schools, opposite the top of Southalls Lane, were opened in 1880. They became a senior mixed school from 1939 and later a county secondary modern school. They closed in 1965 and the school transferred to Wrens Nest Secondary School (later Mons Hill School), also opened in 1965. Demolition commenced in 1965 although some of the buildings on the site still remain, later being used as council offices, and part of the site is now a car park.

Sir Gilbert Claughton School, Blowers' Green Road, probably soon after its opening in 1904. It opened as the Upper Standard School but became the Higher Elementary School in 1912 and the Intermediate School in 1929. It was a secondary school providing education for children over eleven and later twelve, mainly in modern and practical subjects. It gained grammar school status in 1957 and the name was changed to the Sir Gilbert Claughton School. It closed as a school in 1990 and became council offices.

Dudley Grammar School, St James's Road, possibly late 1920s or 1930s. It is believed that the Grammar
School was founded in 1562. The building on this site was opened in 1899. Prior to this the school had
been in various locations including St Edmund's Churchyard, Queen's Cross and Wolverhampton Street.
The school buildings have been extended several times, recently to accommodate Castle High School
formed by the amalgamation of Dudley Grammar School, the Dudley Girls' High School and the Bluecoat
School in 1989. (Valentine & Sons Ltd postcard, published by kind permission of Hallmark Cards)

Dudley Girls' High School, Priory
Road, probably 1950s. The school
opened in 1910 but its origins were
in a private school in a house in
Trinity Road, opened in 1881, which
later moved to larger premises in St
James's Road. The school
amalgamated with Dudley Grammar
School in 1975 and with the Blue
Coat School, to become Castle High
School, in 1989. The school was split
between this site and St James's Road
until the closure and demolition of
this building in 1996. The site is now
a car park.

St Joseph's Roman Catholic School behind the Roman Catholic Church, Portersfield, and included on a photograph taken to show housing conditions in connection with the Birmingham Street Clearance Order, 1930. A new school was built and opened in 1871 under the charge of the Sisters of Charity of St Paul. A site for a new school in Hillcrest Road was acquired in 1972.

The Municipal Technical School, Stafford Street, c. 1915. The school was established in a former board school in Stafford Street, on a site opposite Victoria Street, in 1896 under the aegis of the Technical Instruction Committee. By 1912 commercial subjects were being taught in St James's Road and science subjects on this site. The school was transferred to the Technical College on its opening in March 1936. It was used as ARP headquarters during the war and demolished in 1946–7. The site became part of the Stafford Street car park after 1973.

View of Dudley Training College, entitled 'Castle View from the Hostel' and from a college album of photographs, c. 1915. The college (for training teachers) was opened on 16 July 1905 by the Rt Hon. Walter Runciman, Minister of Education. It became known as Dudley College of Education in 1965 and merged with Wolverhampton Polytechnic in 1976; it is now the Dudley site of Wolverhampton University.

Dudley Technical College, the Broadway, c. 1950. The college was opened in 1936 and was known as Dudley and Staffordshire Technical College. It became Dudley Technical College in 1967. The building still exists although it has been extended. (Valentine & Sons Ltd postcard, published by kind permission of Hallmark Cards)

Children in costume, possibly practising for a school concert at Kates Hill Infants' School. This could be the concert held in May 1931 that is recorded in the school logbook. The photograph includes Jack Ruston, who kindly supplied the original photograph from which this was taken. Left to right: Muriel Stanbie, –?–, Walter Bakewell, Stan Whitehouse, Olive Smart, Jack Ruston, Cliff Wickstead, Eileen Ashwin.

Children at Northfield Road Infants' School, Netherton, rehearsing for the May Day Festival, 1914. We have names for some of the children: Dora Dunn, Irene Cendell, Fred Hill, Lily Davies, Naboth Hill, Jessie Raybould, George Fellows, Billy Potter, Mary Stevens, Jimmy Grainger, Phoebe Roper, Gladys Hill, Albert Brookes, May Willetts, Norah Westwood, Alice Baker, Sidney Cartwright and Sarah Greenfield. The logbook records that in 1914 the May Day Festival was held on 1 May at 10.30. A May queen was chosen in each class. Processions and so on occupied the whole 'Games' time.

Class II at Netherton Brewery School in Brewery Street, outside the school, 1931. Dorothy Biddle (later Mrs Dorothy Hill) who supplied the original photograph is on the extreme right on the back row. Third from right on the front row is Cyril Bates and the girl first from the right on the centre row is Brenda Bush.

Children's activities outside Yew Tree Hills School, Highbridge Road, Netherton, 1953, an example of a modern post-war school. It opened in March 1953 and amalgamated with Netherton C. of E. Middle School in 1989; it is now Netherton C. of E. Primary School.

The Clerks' Training School Day Class, 1916. Note the typewriters. The school was established in 1889 to offer commercial courses, both during the day and in the evening. The day school was to prepare young ladies and youths leaving school to qualify as typists and shorthand writers. By this period it was training young women in particular to be typists during the First World War. The fee was £5 for twelve months' tuition (six days a week) in typing, book-keeping and French. Mr Price, the owner of the school, is the only gentleman seated in the second row. The school was in Wolverhampton Street in 1912 but by 1916 was opposite the fountain in the Market Place (Long Entry). It was still in existence with Mrs F. Price as proprietor in 1940 at 259a Castle Street.

CHAPTER SIX

TRANSPORT

One of Netherton's first cars outside the Star Inn, 1909, with some of the customers of that pub, which closed in 1917. The publican, Tommy Dunn, is in the front passenger seat. The car is a Standard, registered in September 1909 probably to Thomas Baker & Co., of Castle Garage, Dudley, for trade purposes, and painted blue with red lines. Castle Garage was, at this time, Dudley's sole agent for BSAs, Minervas, Darracqs and Standard cars, and also advertised vehicles for hire. So perhaps the car was rented for an excursion – hence the photograph and blackboard.

A steam-powered tram, Tipton Road, *c.* 1904. The earliest trams were horse-drawn, but these were converted to steam engines in the 1880s and a number of new lines were opened. The tall chimney was intended to carry the smoke and smuts over the upper deck. By the time this photograph was taken steam was already being phased out in favour of electricity, and the numerous small tram operators were being swallowed up by the British Electric Traction Company.

A double-decker electric tram in Wolverhampton Street, early 1900s. Perhaps this is a coronation or jubilee since the union flag is much in evidence. The first electric tram ran in Dudley on 25 July 1899 and within two years services were operating to Netherton, Old Hill, Cradley Heath, Sedgley, Kingswinford and Wolverhampton as well as some steam services still being in operation.

The last Dudley to Stourbridge tram, 1930. By 1915 trams ran on this line as frequently as every seven minutes, on a Saturday night. The last tram in Dudley ran on 30 September 1939 on the Oldbury route. The decision to phase out trams and replace them with buses, which were more versatile, had been taken ten years before.

A Wolverhampton to Dudley trolley bus in Stone Street, 1960s. These electric buses began running in Dudley in 1923. The first service from Wolverhampton into Dudley ran on 8 July 1927 and by the mid-1960s they ran every five minutes. When the last one ran on 5 March 1967 people queued at Wolverhampton to catch it, and each passenger received a card which read: 'In Affectionate Remembrance of the Wolverhampton Trolley buses which succumbed to the effects of diesel fumes'! The following day motor buses began operating on the old trolley bus routes.

A Great Western Railway saddle tank engine on the Darby End to Dudley line, 1901. The railway reached Dudley in 1850, when the South Staffordshire Railway connected Dudley to Wednesbury. The line was opened to goods traffic in March, with great festivities. The passenger line opened in May, much more quietly. The main Oxford, Worcester and Wolverhampton line which ran through Dudley and Blowers Green took a further two years to complete. In 1901 the cost of a return ticket to travel from Dudley to Birmingham ranged from 2s for first class, to 1s 5d for third class.

Dudley station, 1956. The station opened in 1850. When its closure was announced in 1963, it dealt with seventy-three passenger trains each day. It officially closed to passengers on 14 June 1964, when the last train left for Birmingham Snow Hill, but the Walsall line remained open until 4 July. The final passenger train was a special excursion from Nottingham to Dudley Zoo on the August bank holiday. In anticipation of an influx of nostalgic travellers, BR put extra carriages on for the final Dudley to Birmingham run, but in fact fewer than fifty people travelled in each direction.

A goods train approaching Blowers Green station, 1956. The station opened in 1878 and stood about a mile to the south-west of Dudley, at the junction between the Windmill End branch line to Old Hill and the West Midlands line to Stourbridge. It was originally called Dudley (South Side) and Netherton, but was renamed Blowers Green in 1921. When the passenger service to Stourbridge was withdrawn in 1962 Blowers Green station was closed, although trains to Old Hill continued to pass through, without stopping, until that line also closed in 1968.

The entrance to Dudley Canal Tunnel, Tipton Road, 1966. The tunnel, opened in 1792, connected the Dudley and Birmingham canal systems. In 1853 more than 40,000 boats passed through the tunnel, but by 1950, when it was closed to commercial traffic, only five boats a week were using it. Dudley Tunnel was officially closed by Act of Parliament in 1962, but largely thanks to members of Dudley Canal Trust it was partially reopened on 21 April 1973.

Legging through Dudley Tunnel. Dudley Tunnel is narrow, with no towpaths, so the only means of propulsion in the early days was for the bargees to lie on their backs and push against the roof with their feet, while the horses were led over the top. It is said that it took about four hours to leg a fully laden narrow boat through the 3,154-yard tunnel.

'Dudley Dig-In' cruise, October 1971. Dudley Canal Trust and Friends of the Black Country Museum organised numerous volunteers in the early 1970s to carry out restoration work on Dudley's canals. On this occasion the party concentrated on the area around the Tipton entrance to Dudley Tunnel. The narrow boats in the picture are 'Laurel' of Netherton, in front, and 'George'. Cobb's engine house can be seen in the background, which places this stretch of canal right on the old boundary of Dudley.

A horse-drawn narrow boat emerges from Netherton Tunnel at Darby End, 1955. Netherton Tunnel was opened in 1858, to relieve the congestion in Dudley Canal Tunnel, and was the last canal tunnel to be built in Britain. It connects Windmill End and Tipton, and most of it is outside the old Dudley county borough. The tunnel is 3,027 yards long, marginally shorter than Dudley, 24 ft high and 27 ft across, with a towpath on both sides. The canal itself, at 17 ft wide, is the largest underground channel in Britain.

The Sounding Bridge, Netherton, c. 1935. This bridge over Dudley No. 2 Canal was built in 1858 to replace a tunnel, hence the rock sides. Its official name is High Bridge, but it is generally known as the Sounding Bridge because of the quality of the echoes produced underneath it. At 60 ft high, it is one of the highest canal bridges in the Midlands, and as such has a somewhat macabre history as a favoured site for suicides. The cottage on the left belonged to the canal company, and Lodge Farm reservoir is behind it.

Sumner's Garage, on the corner of Stourbridge Road and Kingswinford Road, Holly Hall, 1930s. The proprietor at this time was Elias Sumner, who was in business there during the 1920s and '30s. It seems that the business was both a motor repair garage and also a filling station. An advertisement for Avon Tyres is clearly visible in the background. It is interesting that each pump has a different oil company's name on it. The site is currently unoccupied.

Broadway Garage, The Broadway, *c.* 1936. In 1935 this garage advertised as official agents for and specialists in Morris, Singer, Wolseley, Vauxhall and Citroen cars. Percy Whittingham had only recently moved his car sales business to this impressive new showroom. Previously he had managed a garage in New Street and later Downing Street, and a service station at Burnt Tree. Percy Whittingham retired in 1952 and died in Cornwall in 1966. The Broadway Garage, however, continued to trade until the early 1980s.

Two views of the roads around Birmingham Road bus garage, 3 July 1951. The photograph above shows Tipton Road and Station Bridge, while the other is of Birmingham Road itself. The bus depot is the building on the right of both pictures, with the columned frontage. It opened on 2 August 1929, and could accommodate fifty vehicles, as well as having workshops and a bookings and enquiry office on site. It is said that the building was not well designed for its purpose, and that much manoeuvring and reversing was required to park buses inside, which led to a number of accidents over the years. It is clear from these pictures that traffic congestion was already a problem in the area, even in the early 1950s. The bus garage was demolished in 1994 to make way for the Dudley southern bypass.

Burnt Tree traffic island, Birmingham Road, on the borough boundary, under construction in 1952.
Traffic on this stretch of road had been getting progressively heavier: a road census in 1934 recorded a
peak of 1,114 vehicles between 5 p.m. and 6 p.m. on a Monday. Work did not begin on the new traffic
island until 1951. It was officially opened by the Parliamentary Secretary to the Minister of Transport in
September 1952, although it had been in use for some weeks before. The ceremony was kept short, partly
because of the rain, but also so as to keep traffic disruption to a minimum. The total cost of the project
was £30,000 and the finished roundabout was the largest in the Midlands, measuring 200 ft across at its
widest point. By 1963 congestion had become so severe that the borough council petitioned the Ministry
of Transport to build an underpass to carry the Birmingham New Road. This was rejected, but the idea
was still being debated in the 1970s. Finally, in the 1980s, the island was reduced in size to improve traffic
flow and reduce accidents.

CHAPTER SEVEN

INDUSTRY

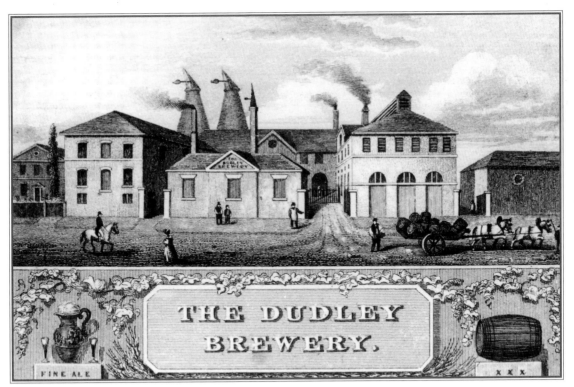

The Dudley Brewery: an engraving of the plant from Birmingham and Its Vicinity as a Manufacturing
and Commercial District *by William Hawkes Smith, 1836. The brewery in Birmingham Road was
established by a consortium of local businessmen in 1805. It ceased production between 1857 and 1869
when the premises were sold. The malthouse survived until 1919 when housing development began, a
reminder of the brewery's existence being the Brewery Fields Estate.*

Limestone quarry on the west side of the Wrens Nest, photograph by J. Rhodes, Geological Survey, 1921. Limestone was mined, particularly on Castle Hill and the Wrens Nest, for household and agricultural purposes, building stone and later as a flux in iron production. Local limestone was used for buildings at Dudley Castle from the seventeenth century. Production had ceased by 1924, although the lime kilns on the west side of the hill continued until 1935 using limestone from Much Wenlock in Shropshire.

Seven Sisters Caverns on the Wrens Nest, photographed for the Dudley County Borough Official Guide, 1960. This was one of the extensive caverns left under Castle Hill and the Wrens Nest after the extraction of limestone; it was named after the seven stone pillars left to support the roof. Wrens Nest Hill was declared a National Nature Reserve in 1956 in recognition of the importance of the site as a source of Silurian age fossils – the first reserve recognised in the United Kingdom for geological reasons. One noteworthy fossil was the Dudley locust, which formed part of the county borough's coat of arms.

Coal and clayworking on land adjoining the Dudley Workhouse, built in 1859, which later became Burton Road Hospital. This is one of a series of photographs of areas on the northern boundary of Dudley adjoining Sedgley, possibly taken in connection with Dudley's proposals for boundary extensions in 1928. The photographs were taken from the 'main road', probably the Dudley to Sedgley road. It shows a gin pit (also found in other areas) where the tubs of coal from shallow workings with no problems of flooding were pulled up by a horse travelling in a circle round a rope drum. Burton Road Hospital was demolished in 1994 and the area was used for housing.

Group of colliers at one of the Dibdale Collieries, possibly Russells Hall, probably between 1870 and 1890. It includes the winding gear, tramway rails (for transporting the coal) and pit ponies. Joseph Smith is believed to be one of the middle two men of the group, the other being Jako, surname unknown.

Group of colliers in front of the wooden pit head gear at Netherton No. 8 Pit, c. 1910. These photographs illustrate the coal mining industry formerly widespread in the area but now disappeared entirely. There was mining of coal from the thirteenth century, but by the end of the nineteenth century many mines had been worked out and there were problems with flooding. The last mine in the area was Baggeridge, outside Dudley, which opened in 1912 and closed in 1968.

Netherton Side Welders (Chain-makers) in the factory of N. Hingley and Sons Ltd, taken from *The Souvenir of the Semi-Jubilee of the Chainmakers and Strikers Association*, 1914. The firm was established in 1837 and introduced anchor manufacturing, in addition to wrought iron and chainmaking, in 1848. It supplied ships' anchors, chains and chain cables for many large ships. It seems ironic that inland Dudley should have been a centre of anchor manufacturing, but this was because of the excellence of the iron. The firm closed in 1980 and the site is now a trading estate.

The anchor for the White Star liner the *Titanic* being transported by a team of twenty horses from the manufacturers, N. Hingley and Sons Ltd of Netherton on 1 May 1911 to the London & North Western Railway station at Dudley (the goods station on the opposite side of Tipton Road to Dudley station). From there it was taken to Fleetwood and then on to Belfast, to the builders, Harland & Wolff. At this time it was the 'biggest Anchor in the World', weighing 16 tons. The costings for the anchor and the patent still survive.

Lloyds British Testing House Co. Ltd, Proving House, Cradley Road, Netherton, *c.* 1929, showing the examination and testing of chain and the office. The importance of testing chain and its material was realised at the beginning of the nineteenth century. The first public test house for chains in the Black Country was set up in Tipton in 1864, and another proving house was established in Cradley Road in 1865. From 1863 testing houses were under the supervision of the Lloyds Register of Shipping, controlling the testing and ensuring its independence. The proving house closed in about 1992.

Brick kilns at the Stourbridge Glazed Brick and Fire Clay Co. Ltd, Thornleigh Works, Blowers Green, photograph by J. Rhodes for the Geological Survey, 1921. The firm (later known as SGB Co. Ltd) was established in 1892 and closed in about 1966–7. It manufactured wall and floor tiles, glazed bricks, fireplaces and sanitary ware besides firebricks. It was one of the firms exploiting the fireclay deposits in the area.

Group of workers at Wilkinsons, anvil makers, Kates Hill, *c.* 1918. Thomas White is third from the right. The firm of Joshua Wilkinson, jnr (Dudley) Ltd, Freebodies Works, St John's Road, manufacturers of anvils, vices, hammers, picks, smiths' tools, shovels, spades and so on had been established in 1830 according to a trade catalogue of about 1901. The firm seems to have closed between 1924 and 1928. Anvils and vices had been made in Dudley by a number of companies since the seventeenth century, the best known of which possibly being Wrights, which exported large numbers to the United States of America.

General view of the works of Old Park Engineering Ltd, photographed for the Dudley County Borough Official Guide, 1960 edition. Old Park Engineering, which manufactured welded steel fabrications, opened a purpose-built factory at Holly Hall in 1957. The factory was taken over by Simon Engineering (Dudley) Ltd in 1975 and closed in 1994 when production was relocated to Gloucester. The building is currently occupied by Servosteel Ltd.

The interior of an unidentified wheelwright's shop, photographed by E. Blocksidge, *c.* 1920. In 1921 there were two firms of wheelwrights listed as being in Dudley: John Baker of Queens Cross and Wellington Road and Edward Evans, 49 and 50 Steppingstone Street. This could be a photograph of the latter firm. Edward Evans moved from Netherton in 1890 to take over an already established business of wheelwrights and coach builders. In the beginning the firm was mainly concerned with horse-drawn vehicles but became increasingly concerned with motor vehicles. The firm moved to Bath Street in 1967.

Offices of Harper Sons & Bean Ltd (makers of the Bean car), Waddams Pool, *c.* 1919–20. The car, registration FD 1184, was registered on 18 December 1919 to the firm. This is possibly a posed photograph taken for publicity to mark the beginning of production. A consortium was formed to manufacture cars in 1919, with members including Harper Sons & Bean Ltd, ironfounders. The cars were assembled in Tipton and then driven to Dudley for body-finishing. Production was transferred to Tipton in 1927 and ceased in 1934.

Blocksidge's Printing Works, 1902, showing the printing machines and a handbill advertising Blocksidge's *Dudley Almanack* for 1901. E. Blocksidge (Dudley) Ltd, printers and stationers of 20 Stone Street, was established by Edwin Blocksidge in 1872 and carried on by his family after his death in 1909. Edwin Blocksidge commenced the series of Dudley Almanacks in 1878 and they were published annually from 1881 until 1951–2, with a gap from 1916 to 1925; they include historical as well as topical information. The firm was taken over by the Herald Press in 1939 and seems to have ceased trading in about 1962.

Composing room at the Herald Press (publisher of the *Dudley Herald* and associated newspapers), photographed for the *Dudley Herald* Centenary Supplement, 1966. The first issue of the *Dudley Herald* was published on 22 December 1866 by Samuel Mills, a jobbing printer, and was based at 210 Wolverhampton Street. The paper moved to premises in Priory Street in 1907 or 1908. The firm became Hepworth Press in 1971 and printing was moved to Walsall in 1974. The *Herald* became a free paper in 1980 but ceased publication in 1982. The premises became an old persons' home, Herald Court, in 1983 – preserving the name.

Engraving by E. Blocksidge, *c.* 1920. This was possibly made as publicity material for Town Mills Ltd, proprietors Grainger & Smith Ltd, and depicted the factory in New Mill Street. The Town Mills factory was built in 1901 to manufacture clothing. Grainger & Smith traded as wholesale woollen merchants, manufacturing clothiers and wholesale outfitters in High Street and King Street and later New Mill Street. In 1951 a new branch factory was opened in Cannock. This was extended in 1961, when the premises in Dudley were sold and operations concentrated in Cannock. The Dudley factory were demolished in 1969.

Machine room at Messrs Wentworth, wholesale clothing manufacturers, King Street, possibly 1950s or 1960s. The firm was established by 1916 when James Wentworth, described as a tailor, was at the address. It had become a wholesale clothing manufactory by 1921. The firm closed in 1981. These two photographs provide examples of clothing manufacture, for which Dudley was well known from the middle of the nineteenth century.

CHAPTER EIGHT

SHOPS & SERVICES

No. 106 Queens Cross, pre-1911. A compulsory purchase order was served on the property on 14 January 1960 and it was subsequently demolished to make way for the landscaping in front of the high-rise flats. Many local shops were, like this one, residential properties where the front room had been converted into a shop selling sweets, tobacco and groceries. Changing shopping patterns have led to the demise of small corner shops; today's shopper buys in bulk and wants a wider choice of goods at cheap prices, leading to the growth of supermarkets and out-of-town shopping developments.

No. 77 Flood Street, 1930s. This general store was owned by the Barrington family for three generations. The photograph shows a group in the doorway and includes Hilda Barrington (now Mrs Pettifer) aged fourteen at the front with her mother Nellie on the right, the two other ladies being customers. Electoral rolls reveal the Barrington family at that address until 1934, and then from 1936 to 1954 the Morris family.

No. 6 Castle Street. This leather and shoe shop was purchased with a number of adjacent properties by Dudley Council, and demolished in 1933 to allow road widening in Castle Street between St Edmund's Church and Fisher Street to take place. The proprietor at this time was Joseph Smith who is shown on this photograph.

Ernest Appleton in the doorway of his pet shop in Portersfield, 1936. Appleton initially worked in his father's tailoring business in Porter Street, but in the 1930s opened up in the front two rooms of this building. As a tongue-in-cheek gesture he commissioned commercial photographer C.N.F. Lewis to take this print advertising his pet shop as 'The Original Dudley Zoo', prior to the opening of Dudley Zoo. When the Portersfield area was cleared in about 1938–9 Appleton moved to a new development at the junction of King Street and Union Street. (Information and photograph are courtesy of F. Power)

No. 1 Hall Street, 1958. During December 1958 this former Burton's shop was fitted up as a temporary branch library and display centre. Its aim was to bring to the attention of Dudley people the services offered by Dudley Public Libraries by using the large windows to display books for lending, together with details of other resources and services available. By 1964 the property had been demolished, presumably as part of the Hall Street development project.

Cook's, High Street, *c.* 1895–1900. Samuel Cook, chartist and dissenter, founded his drapery business on 8 May 1819 at Gibraltar House, 78 High Street. These premises had been owned by George Jones and Cook married his only daughter. In 1844 Cook's son, Samuel Quartus Cook, became a partner and the firm traded as Samuel Cook & Son. After Samuel Cook's death in 1861, his son traded solely in plain goods, selling the business in 1884 to his youngest son F.W. Cook, who later purchased nos 75–76 and 79–80. Each shop was to be devoted to a different class of business.

F.W. Cook Ltd, High Street, 1969. Mr Cook purchased these buildings on the opposite side of the road and extended them back to King Street, opening them as a furnishing business. He travelled extensively, bringing back new ideas for the shop from Europe and America. In 1957 Geoffrey N. Cook, the great grandson of the founder, took over as chairman and oversaw a complete reorganisation, but in 1985 Cook's was closed as a department store, becoming a new-style store that sold concessions to specialist traders. Renovation work has been recently carried out and the premises are now occupied by J.C.'s Stores.

Betteridge's, pawnbroker and jeweller, New Street, photographed between 1900 and 1910. The firm was listed in Blocksidge's *Dudley Almanack* as trading at 37 (later 14) New Street from 1894 to 1946–7. The houses in New Street were re-numbered in 1934 following demolition of many properties because of planned street widening (no. 37 became no. 14). During the 1940s the premises appear to have been taken over by Henn's Jewellers. An obituary for Julia Betteridge in March 1945 refers to her as 'the wife of A.G. Betteridge, former proprietor of an old established jewellery business in New Street'. The premises are now occupied by Rees Page Solicitors.

E.C. Theedam Ltd, High Street, early nineteenth century. Theedam acquired these ironmongery premises in 1885, and in 1886 a site at New Mill Street for manufacturing sheet metal and colliery equipment. Premises at Churchfield Street were purchased in the 1920s, but sold in 1970 when the business was transferred to King Street. The High Street store was refurbished following a fire in 1951 and a trade counter opened at the rear. It was sold for re-development in about 1973 or 1974, and the company now trades from Gainsborough House, Vicar Street. Edward Charles Theedham retained his business interests until his death in 1936 aged eighty-four.

This advert of about 1912 for Rhodes Steam Bakery shows a line of horse-drawn delivery vehicles outside the Eagle Bakery, 53b Stafford Street. Solomon Rhodes was a grocer and provision merchant at 144–5 Wolverhampton Street, almost opposite the junction with Stafford Street. By 1926 the Eagle Bakery was owned by W. Price & Sons and a rate book of 1929–33 shows the owner initially as Price & Sons, but amended to show the later owners as 'Daily Bread Ltd'. The premises were still shown as a bakery on the 1963 OS map, but by 1972 the premises were shown as 'Works'.

Lloyds Old Bank, 25 Wolverhampton Street, c. 1866–76. The bank was formerly known as Lloyds, Barnetts and Bosanquet Bank Ltd, and Lloyds Bank Ltd from 1890. This building was referred to as Lloyds Old Bank and demolished in 1876; the new bank was erected on the same site and is still there today. This picture shows the manager George Wilkinson JP in the carriage. Wilkinson was the manager from 1866 to 1898 when he retired; he was also the Borough Treasurer from 1865 to 1902, and treasurer for the Guest Hospital and the Dudley Institute. He was succeeded as manager of Lloyds Bank by J. Nichols.

The Worcestershire Furnishing Company, 211–212 Wolverhampton Street, *c.* 1910, showing J. Astley, shop manager, standing outside the store. This company traded initially as the Worcestershire Furnishing Co., later as Goodlys Furnishing Company, then Goodlys Ltd, until the 1960s. The site has been occupied by the Yorkshire Bank since about 1982. The store originated in Dudley, with branches in Bradford, Manchester and Leicester, and its head office was in Birmingham. The proprietor visited each store weekly. A weekly easy-payment scheme was offered, so working people could afford to purchase furnishings: in 1890 goods worth up to £2 10s 0d could be bought for 2s 6d per week.

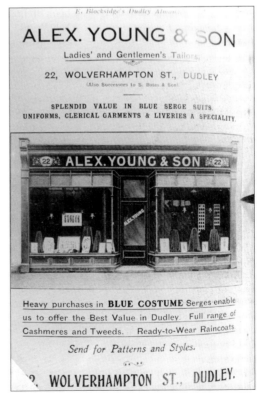

Alex. Young & Son, 22 Wolverhampton Street, advert from Blocksidge's *Dudley Almanack*, 1914. Alex Young appears to have started in business as a tailor and draper in Stafford Street in the late 1870s, later moving to 12 Wolverhampton Street then to 22 Wolverhampton Street in about 1909. In 1940 the company was listed at 23 Stone Street where it remains. Alex Young, a councillor and JP, died in 1922 aged seventy-three after a long illness. He lived in Dudley all his life and was very active in politics and public life, having a keen interest in education and social welfare issues.

General Post Office, Wolverhampton Street, 1911. Before 1879 Dudley's post office operated from a shop at 22 Wolverhampton Street. At this time Dudley had two post boxes, five postmen and two office clerks. In 1879 the present post office headquarters on the junction of Priory Street and Wolverhampton Street were erected, then enlarged in 1891. Further extensions were made in 1909 when the red brick façade was replaced with the present stone frontage, Dudley Council offering £400 towards the cost. Work was completed on the building in 1911. The post office was transferred to premises at 237–8 High Street in the mid-1980s.

This photograph of the post office workers, dated 1926, includes W.H. Harper, aged sixteen, the messenger boy. He is the tallest figure on the back row.

Advert for Palethorpe's sausages, probably 1880s. The firm was originally founded as a pork butchery by Henry Palethorpe in 1852 at Gooch Street, Birmingham. In 1873 he moved to Market Place, Dudley, and following competition from American hams expanded into the manufacture of sausages. 'Royal Cambridge' sausages enjoyed a world-wide reputation and the firm also produced pork pies, pressed beef, etc. Henry died in 1880 and the business was taken over by his son Charles Henry Palethorpe; rapid expansion followed and the firm moved to larger premises at Dudley Port in about 1890, where it remained until 1966.

Fountain Arcade, Market Place, 1958. The arcade was the brainchild of Alderman T.W. Tanfield, proprietor of the Fountain Stationery Co., who lived in Tower Street. Building work started in 1925: the architect was George Coslett; the builders were A.J. Crump and Mark Round. The building was constructed on a steel framework faced with glazed terracotta. Measuring 15 ft by 270 ft, the arcade had a glass roof and a marble mosaic pavement; it was opened by Mrs Tanfield in 1926. The building was purchased from the Tanfield Trust in 1963, and the new owners (Bena Estates Ltd) undertook a modernisation project between 1964 and 1969.

Birdcage Walk, photographed here in 1967, was officially opened on 17 April 1964 by Alderman G.B. Norton. The building of this covered pedestrian walkway between 1962 and 1964 was the first phase of the Churchill Centre redevelopment. It was designed by the Borough Architect, J.T. Lewis, taking its name from an aviary housing tropical birds erected on 7 August 1964 at one end. In 1981 C&A opened a shop on the former car park; it closed in 1992 and the premises were taken over by Kwik Save the same year.

Churchill Precinct, 1984. Opened on 8 September 1969 by Viscount Cobham, the precinct was the third stage of the redevelopment of the Hall Street/King Street area, which cost Dudley Council about £550,000 in total. It provided a safe, up-to-date shopping centre, with pedestrian-only access. Its most striking feature was this 40-ft-wide Churchill Screen sculpted by Bainbridge Copnall, consisting of seventeen glass panels illustrating the life of Winston Churchill. The portrait was removed owing to weather damage and vandalism in 1984–5, and the remainder during the early 1990s. In 1992 the Council sold the precinct to LCP who have recently refurbished it.

CHAPTER NINE

PUBLIC HOUSES & CINEMAS

The Locomotive Inn, Trindle Road, c. 1910. The pub, owned by Jackson's stood behind Fairground Field, probably from around the time Dudley railway station opened. Its licence was removed in 1955, as the magistrates felt that there was no need for it. The police evidence stated that there were nineteen licensed houses within a radius of 440 yards, and on ten visits a police sergeant counted only twenty-six customers in total. The lorries pictured outside belong to A. Harper Sons & Bean Ltd, iron founders and engineers of Waddams Pool, who later made Bean cars.

The Seven Stars Inn, Market Place, 1954. At that time it was the second oldest surviving inn in Dudley, having been licensed since 1634/5. The oldest was the Old Woolpack, licensed thirteen years earlier. Originally the Seven Stars fronted on to Hall Street, but in the mid-nineteenth century new buildings were erected in front of it, so it became part of High Street. Ansell's, the owners of the Seven Stars, closed it in about 1960, saying that the space was not available to reconstruct it as a modern pub. The Woolpack had been closed a little earlier.

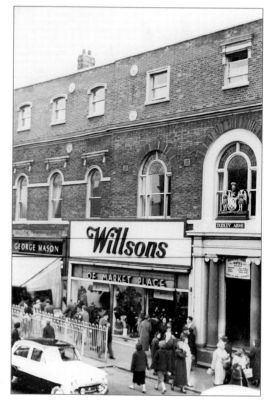

The Dudley Arms Hotel, Market Place, 1957. There had been an inn on this site since the seventeenth century. The original Rose and Crown was replaced with the Dudley Arms in 1786. It was for many years Dudley's principal coaching inn. The Dudley Arms was demolished in 1968, despite having listed status, to allow the neighbouring Marks & Spencer's to expand. The coat of arms was given to the fledgling Dudley Industrial Museum (later the Black Country Museum) and a large stained glass window from the staircase found a new home in the Talbot Hotel, Stourbridge.

The Saracen's Head and Freemasons' Arms Hotel, Stone Street, Dudley, also known as 'The Napper',
c. 1890s. This was one of the town's important coaching inns. It was originally named in commemoration
of the crusades, and became the headquarters for the freemasons' lodge, hence the addition to its name.
Beer was brewed on the premises until 1881. Julia Hanson's father, John Mantle, was licensee of the
Saracen's Head between 1835 and 1850, although his son Reuben ran it for much of this time, while John
was landlord at the Stewponey and Foley Arms at Kinver. Julia married Thomas Hanson in 1846, and in
the following year they established a wine and spirit business in Dudley. It was based in Priory Street and
may have been part of the Saracen's Head buildings. Thomas Hanson died in 1870 and Julia continued to
run the business. It was during her time at the helm that Hanson's became a brewery as well as a wine and
spirit merchant. Julia Hanson died in 1894, but her sons carried on the business as Julia Hanson & Sons;
they purchased the Saracen's Head in the early 1900s. Hanson's later became part of the Wolverhampton
and Dudley Brewery. The Saracen's Head still stands and has changed little, although a conservatory has
recently been added on the left-hand side, and the frontage is now almost obscured by trees. It is now part
of the Banks' Brewery chain.

The King and Queen public house on the corner of Southalls Lane and Stafford Street, *c*. 1900. The licensee, George Biddle, can be seen on the right. It was bought by Wolverhampton and Dudley Brewery in 1909 and survived, in a new building, until the early 1990s.

The Hammer Inn, Stafford Street, between 1913 and 1921. As the signs show, this was a home brew pub. The beer was known as 'Bullock's Blood', apparently after William Bullock, who was the licensee between 1873 and 1901. The Hammer was sold to Ansell's in 1938 and closed in the 1960s.

The White Swan, Baptist End, and its customers, *c.* 1910. This was another home brew pub, which was owned by the Roe family from the 1880s until 1939. Mary Ann Roe's name can be seen above the door here and it was she who eventually sold the inn to Holt's/Ansell's.

The Station Inn at the corner of Shaw Road and Hope Street, Netherton, 1920s. The beer prices in the window make interesting reading – mild at 5*d* a pint and bitter at 7*d*! Like the Locomotive this pub probably dates from about 1850. It was built and owned, until the 1890s, by Solomon Danby, who was also a coffin maker. After his death it was leased to Matthew Smith, and bought by J.F.C. Jackson, of the Diamond Brewery in Kates Hill in 1912. It survived until 1978.

The Old Swan, Halesowen Road, Netherton, 1980s. This pub is famous for still brewing its own beer. Its popularity is evident from the sign on the wall: 'Coaches by Appointment Only'! It is known locally as Ma Pardoe's after its most famous licensee, Doris (Ma) Pardoe, who with her husband took over in 1932, bought the freehold in 1964 and continued to run the pub until her death in 1984. The Pardoes never brewed beer themselves but employed first Solomon Cooksey and then his son George – largely because Mr Cooksey senior refused to pass his recipe on to anyone else!

The Angel, Castle Street, before 1935, when it was rebuilt. Edward Elcock Jones, father of Doris (Ma) Pardoe, held the licence here between 1915 and 1918. Bought by W. Butler in 1959, the Angel eventually became part of the Mitchell and Butler chain.

The Opera House on Castle Hill, *c.* 1900. The theatre had opened on 4 September 1899 with *The Mikado*. It was founded, owned and managed by John Maurice Clement who had also built the Colosseum next door. The Colosseum went through a number of subsequent name changes, becoming the Gem, the John Bull and the Scala, before being demolished in the 1930s when it was replaced with a purpose-built cinema, the Plaza, which finally closed in 1990 and was demolished in 1997.

The Opera House was said to be the most modern theatre of its day but sadly, it burnt to the ground in November 1936. By this time its owner was Benjamin Kennedy, who had reopened the Plaza next door only about five months previously. The scale of the destruction can be seen here.

Dudley Hippodrome interior, 1957. This new theatre was built on the site of the Opera House and opened on 19 December 1938. It could seat about 1,700 people, and claimed to be the first provincial theatre to present Bob Hope and Laurel and Hardy, and also the first to televise a pantomime – *Cinderella* in 1951. In 1958 the Kennedy brothers, who had managed the Hippodrome since its opening, decided to sell, blaming higher wage demands from performers for their losses. However, it continued to operate as a live theatre until 1964. It is now a bingo hall.

Castle Hill, showing the Hippodrome and the Plaza, 1950s. On the left is the Station Hotel with the fountain and drinking trough in front of it. Erected in 1862 at the top of Castle Street, to refresh horses after the long pull up the hill from the station, the drinking trough was moved to the junction of Trindle Road and Castle Hill in 1888 to make way for the Earl of Dudley's statue. The fountain was removed in 1962 when road improvements were carried out.

The Odeon on Castle Hill, 1960. This was the last cinema built in Dudley and is in a simple 1930s style. It opened on 28 July 1937 with *The Beloved Enemy* starring Merle Oberon and Brian Ahern. The Odeon's first manager was Charles Crathorn who later became a radio and TV personality. It ceased to be a cinema in 1975, but Dudley Council rejected the Rank Organisation's application to demolish it. The building underwent conversion in 1976 and is now used as a Jehovah's Witness Kingdom Hall.

The Empire Cinema building, 1959. It was opened in 1903 as the Dudley New Empire Palace of Varieties but became a full-time cinema in 1912, Dudley's largest, with a capacity of 2,000. It was known for a while as Bosco's Picture Pavilion but became the Empire again after the First World War. It was eventually sold to Denman Picture Houses, a subsidiary of Gaumont British, and closed on 2 November 1940. The building was later used as a Home Guard training centre and then a warehouse. It was demolished in 1975 and a Cousin's furniture store now occupies the site.

The Criterion cinema, 1957. The Criterion started out as a small music hall in King Street, becoming a cinema in 1911. In 1913 the auditorium was extended towards Market Place. Soon after, the old building was replaced with a purpose-built cinema, with its own café above, and the management kept the Criterion open throughout. The last film was shown here in 1956. The front of the Criterion on Market Place became a shop and still stands today, while the rear, facing on to King Street, became a warehouse, and was demolished in 1980.

The Savoy Cinema, Northfield Road, Netherton, 1956. Designed by Stanley Griffiths of Stourbridge, this cinema opened on 26 August 1936. There was no balcony and the auditorium only seated about 500. It is said that many regular attenders expected to have the same seat on each visit! When the Savoy closed on Christmas Eve 1960 it was the only independently owned cinema still operating in Dudley, and Charles Bishop, one of the original directors, was still secretary of the company. Its closure made the front page of the *Dudley Herald*.

CHAPTER TEN

LEISURE

A humorous postcard sent from Dudley Skating Rink, c. 1927. Dudley's first roller-skating rink opened in 1909 in Trindle Road, and by the following Christmas its hockey team had been invited to represent England at the International World Championship in Paris. Unfortunately this rink was destroyed by fire in June 1924. A further successful rink was already in operation, though, in Tipton Road. Dudley's last roller-skating rink, the Savoy in Castle Hill, closed in 1962.

Dudley Football Club in their first season in the Birmingham League, 1898/9. They played at this time at Shavers End, on a ground behind the Struggling Man Inn. The pitch was improved when the team joined the Birmingham League, but when Dudley beat Brierley Hill by 8 goals to 2 in the first round of the 1899 FA Cup, it was found to be 10 yards shorter than it should have been according to the FA's regulations! This, along with the ground's distance from the town centre, led the team to move in 1911 to the county cricket ground. The club closed down in 1915.

Dudley Town FC playing at their home ground on Tipton Road, 1950s. The team, formerly Dudley West End, took over the ground in 1928. Problems with subsidence occurred from the start, but 'The Robins' continued to play here until 1986, when the ground finally had to be abandoned. They then moved to Brierley Hill and played at Round Oak Steelworks' sports and social club until 1996, when the club planned to sell the site for housing. Objections have been raised and so far this has not gone ahead. Dudley Town are not currently playing because of their ground problems.

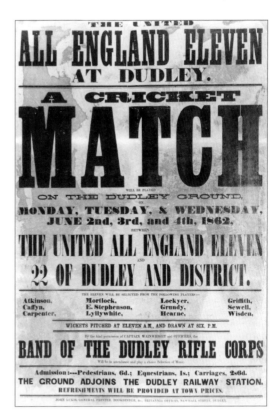

A poster advertising a cricket match between the All England Eleven and a Dudley team of twenty-two in June 1862. The Dudley Cricket Club was only seven years old at the time, so this must have been quite an honour!

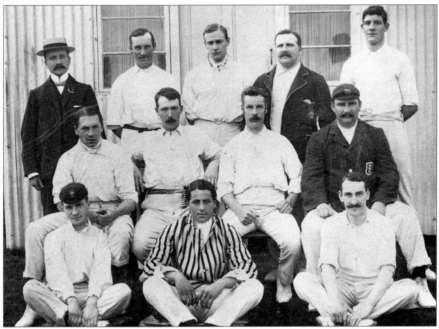

A Dudley team from another era, *c.* 1908. The team seems to have had a professional player at this date, but the pitch was not considered to be county standard. Vigorous fund raising on the part of the club enabled improvements to be carried out and county level cricket came to Dudley after 1913.

Netherton cricket field, 1930s. The cricket club was founded in 1866 and rented this ground from the Earl of Dudley from 1879. The club house, which can be seen in this picture, was given by Samuel Woodhouse, the club's president, at the time of the move. It is based on the design of a Bengali pagoda built for an Indian princess. By the early 1900s the club was prosperous enough to employ a number of professional players, the last of these playing in 1921. The ground was purchased by the club from the Earl of Dudley in 1928.

Grainger & Smith's athletics team, 1909/10. Grainger & Smith was a wholesale woollen merchants established in Dudley in 1870, which eventually became Town Mills Ltd. The company had an athletic ground prepared off Hall Lane, Cinder Bank, Netherton, with a cricket pitch, lawn tennis court and bowling green for the summer and a football pitch for winter. The land was leased from M. and W. Grazebrook and only opened in June 1909, so it would seem that the gentlemen pictured were the first to have use of it.

An ox roast in Stone Street, *c.* 1920. These events were once a popular part of many of the town's celebrations. Priory Street can be seen running along the back of this picture, with the present museum on the corner, next to the *Herald* newspaper offices and the old fire station on the far left. A glasshouse stood near this site until August 1886. It was originally the premises of Dudley Flint Glassworks, founded in 1766, but had not been used since about 1837. By the time of its demolition the glasshouse had become an eyesore and a danger to the public, as parts of it had collapsed. Also, its position narrowed the roadway, creating problems for pedestrians and horse-drawn traffic. The land was then left derelict and a hide and skin market allowed to develop there. This market was filthy and smelly and soon became something of a public nuisance. It was closed down by the corporation in the 1890s, and replaced by the fire station and a wholesale vegetable market.

Blowers Green Road swimming baths at its opening, September 1928. The project had cost a total of £21,550 to complete. Previously the town's swimming baths had been in a former steam flour mill in New Mill Street and had drawn water from the mill pools. The Blowers Green Road baths were closed in January 1976 after freak gales aggravated the building's poor condition. The baths were replaced by a new pool in the sports complex off Wellington Road.

This photograph, entitled 'Health and Beauty', was taken at Dudley Sports Centre, in Birmingham Road, in 1957. Later that year the centre was forced to close because of subsidence. Initially, in August 1957, a large cavern was discovered when the rear wheel of a corporation lorry sank into a hole and it had to be towed out. It was estimated that between 2,000 and 3,000 tons of hard core rubble was required to fill it in. The centre reopened after a week, only to close again at the end of September following further subsidence. The site has since been abandoned.

The fourth annual horse parade and show held by N. Hingley and Sons Ltd and their associated firms on land adjoining Marriott Road, Netherton, 22 June 1929. A crowd of about a thousand gathered to see more than fifty horses compete in the four classes. Only one of these was open to all-comers. The other three categories were open to the firm's employees only. Some incentive to win must have been given by the prize money – up to £3 for the winner of the open class.

Dudley Yacht Club in action on Netherton Reservoir, May 1970. The reservoir was purchased by Dudley Town Council in 1963 for £2,000 from the British Transport Commission. Formerly its sole purpose was to top up the canal, although it was popular with local fishermen. The council immediately leased the reservoir for water ski-ing and sailing for three days each per week. A landing stage, slipway and club house were soon built, the banks landscaped and paved walks laid out. (Picture reprinted courtesy of the News Group)

Two different views of a popular summer pastime. The gentlemen, above, are pictured at Dudley's oldest bowling club – the Conservative Club. The club had its own green at its headquarters in Priory Road, but its use was restricted to members only. By the 1920s bowling had become very popular and Dudley could boast numerous other clubs, including the Waverley Bowling Club on Stourbridge Road, Scotts Green. In 1925 its subscriptions were 21s with an entrance fee of 20s. A ladies' game in progress there in 1957 is pictured below.

The ladies and gentlemen of the Darby End Ramblers' Club on an outing to Haden Hill Park, August 1914. The estate has an interesting history, in that it remained in the same family from shortly after the Norman Conquest until 1876. On the death of the last Haden, Ann Eliza, it passed, briefly, to her half brother, Alfred Haden Barrs, then to his sister, and lastly to her son, George Alfred Haden Haden-Best. At the time of this photograph, the park and house were still in the private ownership of Mr Best, who was, apparently, quite keen to allow local parties to enjoy it. On his death in 1921, Haden Hall and Park were purchased by Rowley Regis Council and now belong to Sandwell MBC. It is hard to imagine that these Dudley visitors intended any serious rambling on this particular day while dressed up so smartly.

The conservatory in Buffery Park, 1960. This is one of the borough's earliest parks, having been laid out in 1891–2. Buffery Park covers an area of 16 acres, purchased by the Corporation in 1891. The aim was to beautify an area which had been scarred by coal and clay extraction, and to provide work for some of Dudley's unemployed residents. The park probably opened in 1913. The policy, in this park as well as others in the borough, has been to emphasise and develop ornamental features, such as this conservatory, as their contours made them largely unsuitable for activities.

The fountain in Netherton Recreation Ground, probably 1930s. The 13 acres or so of this park were purchased by the Corporation from the Earl of Dudley in 1900 for £1,700. It was first used on 26 June 1902 as part of the planned celebrations for the coronation of King Edward VII. The coronation was postponed owing to the king's illness, but 5,573 local children still enjoyed a tea and then adjourned to the park. Most of the other events which should have taken place, in Netherton and elsewhere, were cancelled.

The 5th Dudley Scout Troop, 1913. The first scout troop was formed in Dudley in 1909 and a district committee was established during the following year. When Lord Baden Powell visited Priory Fields at Easter 1910, around 800 scouts from across the South Staffordshire region were present. This photograph was probably taken quite early in this troop's history, since Blocksidge's *Almanack* of 1911 does not list 5th Dudley Scouts among the affiliated troops. It was apparently taken at Scoutmaster Leech's house in Wellington Road.

Bumble Hole Castle or Ziah's Castle, *c.* 1900. This folly was built by Isaiah Chandler and stood in St Peter's Road, opposite the church. The walls were decorated with pieces of sculpture, mosaics, bits of bedsteads and even the dome from the boiler of a locomotive! The garden paths were bordered by sea shells. Mr Chandler and his wife lived in the castle for a number of years and would conduct children around it for a halfpenny, and give them an orange or sweets when they left. This unique building was demolished in the 1920s, and houses were built on the site.

Members of Dudley Golf Club outside their club house, *c*. 1906. Dudley's first golf course was established in 1893, just off Stourbridge Road, but the club moved in the early 1900s to a new course on Himley Road, with a club house near to Grange Park. In the 1920s subsidence caused the club to find a new home and, in 1926, Dudley's first eighteen-hole course was laid out, with six holes on Darby's Hill and twelve on Turner's Hill at Oakham. In the 1960s houses were built on part of the course, but the club survives.

Cradley Heathens speedway team racing at their Dudley Wood Stadium, 1968. The track opened in 1947, but the glory days came in the 1980s and early 1990s, when they won the British League twice and KO cup eight times. In 1994, however, the owners of the stadium announced their plan to sell the site for housing. Objections were raised and the plan rejected. The stadium's owners have, as yet, refused to open it to speedway.

CHAPTER ELEVEN

A CHANGE OF SCENE

Burnt Tree, looking towards the junction of the present Burnt Tree and Tividale Roads, c. 1925. Now, the Birmingham New Road (opened on 2 November 1927 by the Prince of Wales) also converges at this junction, on the Dudley boundary. In 1934 a traffic census was taken at this point, the average hourly number of vehicles being 690 (Monday) and 681 (Tuesday). A traffic island was officially opened here on Saturday 27 September 1952 by Lieutenant-Commander Braithwaite, Parliamentary Secretary to the Minister of Transport.

Above: Market Place from Castle Street, 1959. There has been a market in Dudley since at least 1261, when it was referred to in the Feet of Fines for February 1261–2. The site of the present market is on what was Middle Row, a row of shops down the centre of the High Street, the north-west side being known as Queen Street, culminating at the Old Town Hall. Middle Row was demolished by 1850 and the Old Town Hall in 1860. The Market Place was then cleared, paved and a cab stand erected in 1852. On 17 October 1867 the Earl of Dudley presented the town with a fountain, which was erected on the site of the Old Town Hall. There have been many changes this century, including the removal of the cobblestones and pedestrianisation during 1982–3, the market being temporarily relocated to Stone Street during this time. In the 1990s further refurbishment took place (new street furniture provided, bollards erected and so on) and a new toilet block has been built at the eastern end of the Market Place, now obscuring the view of the market as can be seen in the later photograph, below, taken in 1998.

Above: Fisher Street bus station from Birmingham Street, *c.* 1955. In the foreground is the Trindle Road roundabout and behind it the bus station and the Civic Restaurant. The Civic Restaurant, also known as the Ednam Restaurant, was opened on 29 July 1948 to provide cheap meals, and closed on 29 September 1956 after showing a loss for three years running. The bus station (built at a cost of £16,000) was opened on 27 September 1952 to relieve the traffic congestion from Station Bridge. It was built on a slope, and by the 1970s it was obvious that there was a serious safety problem following numerous minor accidents, and a fatal accident in 1971. In 1981 council approval was given for a new bus station but the project was hit by repeated delays; it was not until about 1987 that the new Fisher Street bus station was opened. The later photograph, taken in 1998, shows this new bus station and the car park that is on the site of the former bus station. The roundabout is now smaller and more elevated.

Above: Flood Street junction with the Minories, 1953. In 1957 Dudley Council submitted proposals to the Ministry of Housing for the development of the Flood Street area at a cost of £350,000. Much of this area had been derelict land for about thirty years (about 450 houses had previously been demolished and the land acquired by the council under slum clearance schemes). The area had been zoned for industry, being deemed unsuitable for mass housing because of the location of the gas works. The council proposed to acquire the remainder through compulsory purchase orders and transform some 27.5 acres into new housing and light industrial developments and several permanent municipal car parks. King Street was to be widened between Flood Street and New Mill Street to have two 22-ft-wide carriageways, and the main access roads to King Street (Flood Street and Constitution Hill) were to be widened to 30 ft. The subsequent Compulsory Purchase Order was dated 1959. The later photograph (1998) shows the widened Flood Street and the car park at the side of the Minories, the building on stilts being Falcon House, former home of the Dudley Health Authority.

Above: Broadway, 1937. The development plans for the Priory Estate contained provision for a bypass along one of its sides linking Dudley (Castle Hill) with Sedgley (Burton Road); this was first considered as early as 1924. The cost was reported to be approximately £25,000. The Broadway was officially opened in a brief ceremony by the mayor, Alderman W.C. Williams, on 1 May 1935; it was not surfaced at this time, however. The contract for surfacing the Broadway and Priory Close was awarded to Messrs John Hatfield & Son on 19 January 1937. There were 287 building sites allocated on the new road, and at the time of opening seventy had already been sold. Certain conditions were laid down to ensure that 'good' types of property were erected and house-building appears to have started as early as 1937 at the Dudley end. On the left-hand side of the 1937 photograph, in the distance, can be seen colliery winding gear, possibly in the Gornal area. The lower photograph shows The Broadway in 1998.

Above: The Inhedge, *c.* 1912. Mrs Ballinger is on the extreme right. These two photographs illustrate the tremendous changes that occurred on The Inhedge. No trace of the pre-Second World War terraced houses is left in 1998 (below). These properties were subject to compulsory purchase under the Old Dock (Dudley) No. 3 CPO of 1960. Demolition took place in the early 1960s and in 1962 a start was made to convert the area between Stafford Street and Cross Street into car parks. In 1971 proposals were put forward for a new magistrates' court, at a cost of £600,000, to replace the old courts in Stafford Street. Work started in February 1973. The Inhedge had to be widened and part of the old burial ground of the Old Meeting House (Unitarian church) was needed for this. The graveyard was not actually built on, but incorporated into the grounds of the magistrates' court. The court was officially opened by Lord Widgery, Lord Chief Justice, on 19 March 1976, although the first case was actually heard in January. In 1984 proposals to develop the corner of The Inhedge and Wolverhampton Street car park were put forward and Inhedge House was built in about 1987. The photograph below shows Inhedge House and the magistrates court in 1998.

Above: Steppingstone Street from the junction with Oxford Street, 1959. Like the Inhedge, properties in Steppingstone Street, Dock Lane and Oxford Street were subject to compulsory purchase under the Old Dock (Dudley) No. 3 CPO of 1960. This was part of the council's massive slum clearance programme of this area. The 1959 photograph shows 'The Terrace' with its distinctive brickwork, at the bottom of Dock Lane on the right-hand side. These were raised terraced houses, built in about 1854–5 by the Dudley branch of the Metropolitan Association for Improving the Dwellings of the Industrious Classes. It is interesting to note the date of 1856 given on the Oxford Street sign, presumably the date the street was built. By 1960 these houses were classed as unfit for human habitation, owing to constant flooding in the cellars, leaking roofs, and communal lavatories and washing facilities. Today much of this area is landscaped or car parking for the Dudley Leisure Centre, which was built in 1978 between Oxford Street and Wellington Road by J. Hickman & Sons of Brierley Hill. Flats have been built on one side of Oxford Street, but Prince Albert Street and Ludgate Street have disappeared. The photograph below shows Steppingstone Street from the junction with Oxford Street in 1998.

Above: Wellington Road from Queens Cross, 1965. The photograph was taken from the junction of Queens Cross and Aston Road, formerly Farthings Lane. The borough cemetery was built on 30 acres of land opposite this junction (behind the photographer) and opened by the mayor, John Hughes, on 30 September 1903. The pram shop on the left-hand side was demolished in the late 1960s, and St Luke's Church on the right-hand side was demolished in 1973. In January 1965 traffic lights were installed in place of a roundabout to improve traffic flow: they were intended to work in conjunction with traffic lights at the Blowers Green junction. An improvement scheme for the A461 at Queens Cross began in 1987, in order to realign the junction, reduce traffic delay by improving road capacity and improve safety for pedestrians. The land required was subject to compulsory purchase, but the later photograph (1998) shows that Jones, monumental mason, is still there – but with improved frontages. The scheme was completed in February 1989 and cost about £2.5 million, although a grant of 50 per cent was given by the European Commission.

Above: Queens Cross at its junction with Blowers Green Road, looking north-west, 1958. The photograph shows Highside, a row of raised eighteenth-century terraced houses. Demolition of some houses took place in 1962; the remainder, together with the embankment and stone wall and footpath running along the top, were demolished in 1965 as part of a proposed road widening scheme for High Street. The area was to be grassed with flower beds and seats installed, and a new footpath built at road level. At this junction was the site of the old Queens Cross cemetery: this was the former burial ground for St Thomas's Church. It was closed in 1937 and taken over by the local authority in 1952, the graves being removed to the borough cemetery and the area used as open space. This junction was altered between 1987 and 1989 as part of the Queens Cross road development scheme, to improve the three road junctions on the A461 between Wellington Road and High Street. The picture below shows the same scene in 1998.

Above: Swan Street, looking east from Prince Street, 1964. The major change to Swan Street occurred when the terraced houses on the left-hand side were demolished in about 1971–2 and replaced by bungalows. Little else has changed: on the left-hand side is still the People's Mission Hall, erected in 1898 by Cooper & Co. of London. This is an undenominational church, originally founded by a breakaway group from the Messiah Baptist church. The Dudley Herald Year Book of 1914 reveals that in that year there were eighty registered members and a hundred children attending the Sunday school. In 1963 the church appointed Lawrence Roddis as its first resident minister; previously it had relied on lay ministers to preach there. The picture below dates from 1998.

Above: Northfield Road, facing north-west from the BR level crossing, 1962. There has been little basic change to Northfield Road between 1962 and 1998; the level crossing has now disappeared, however. This GWR branch line was opened on 10 March 1879 and ran from Windmill End Junction to Withymoor Basin and was known as the Netherton Goods Branch. It closed on 5 July 1965. The turrets of Northfield Road School can be seen on the right-hand side: this school was built in 1891 as Northfield Road Girls and Infants School, becoming a senior mixed school in about 1913, and later Northfield Road Council School. It is now part of Northfield Road Primary School. In the 1998 photograph below, the main change is in the distance on the left-hand side where multi-storey flats have been built. These are the St John Street flats and include Manor Court and Wells Court. The first block was officially opened in February 1966.

ACKNOWLEDGEMENTS

The authors acknowledge their gratitude to the following:

Aerofilms, Allen & Bott, R. Baker, Beddard, A.W. Biddle, Birmingham Post & Mail, T.E. Bredee, British Geological Survey, W. Bullock, Mr Camm, Dudley Cricket Club, Dudley Libraries, Dudley MBC, Dudley Photographic Society members, J. Dunn, *Express & Star*, J.W. Foster, A.R. Guy, Hallmark Cards, Mr and Mrs W.J. Harper, Mrs J. Harris, Mrs D. Hill, Mr and Mrs S. Hill, J. Homery-Folkes, Industrial Photographs Ltd, Mrs O. Jasper, Mrs B. Jones, B. Kennedy, Mr Knowles, C.N.F. Lewis, R.J. Little, W.H. Massey, C.J. Matthews, J.H. Molyneux, The News Group, Mrs I. Orme, M. Payne, Mr Perkins, Mrs M. Pettifer, F. Power, Mrs L. Price, Mr Roberts, R. Round, A. Ruston (St James's, Eve Hill, PCC), Mr Sanford-Smith, F. Siviter, Mrs Stevens, Mrs M. Smith, Mr Somerville, W.H. Sowden, Miss J. Taylor, A. Thompson, Mrs M.A. Tilley, T.S. White.

Especial thanks to members of the Dudley Photographic Society who undertook a photographic survey of Dudley on behalf of the libraries in the 1950s, in particular W. J. Clift, Mr Colley, D.G. Hadlington, R.J. Little, A.B. Mason and W.H. Massey.

Every effort has been made to contact copyright owners and the donors/owners of photographs.

BRITAIN IN OLD PHOTOGRAPHS

Aberdeen
Acton
Amersham
Ashbourne

Around Bakewell
Balham & Tooting
Barnes, Mortlake & Sheen
Barnet & the Hadleys
Barnet Past & Present
Bath
Beaconsfield
Bedfordshire at War
Bedworth
Belfast
Beverley
Bexley
Bideford
Bilston
Bishop's Stortford &
    Sawbridgeworth
Bishopstone & Seaford II
Blackburn
Bletchley
Bloxwich
Braintree & Bocking at Work
Brentwood
Bridgwater & the River
    Parrett
Bridlington
Bristol
Brixton & Norwood
Buckingham & District
Bury
Bushbury

Camberwell, Peckham &
    Dulwich
Cambridge
Cannock Yesterday & Today
Canterbury Cathedral
Canterbury Revisited
Cardigan & the Lower Teifi
    Valley
Around Carlisle
Castle Combe to Malmesbury

Chadwell Heath
Cheadle
Chelmsford
Cheltenham in the 1950s
Cheltenham Races
Chesham Yesterday & Today
Around Chichester
Chiswick & Brentford
Chorley & District
Around Cirencester
Clacton-on-Sea
Around Clitheroe
Colchester 1940–70
Coventry at War
Cowes & East Cowes
Around Crawley
Cromer
Croydon
Crystal Palace, Penge &
    Anerley

Darlington at Work & Play
Darlington II
Dawlish & Teignmouth
Around Devizes
East Devon at War
Dorchester
Dorking Revisited
Dumfries
Dundee at Work
Durham: Cathedral City
Durham People
Durham at Work

Ealing, Hanwell, Perivale &
    Greenford
Ealing & Northfields
The Changing East End
Around East Grinstead
East Ham
Around Eastbourne
Elgin
Eltham
Ely
Enfield

Esher
Exmouth & Budleigh Salterton
Farnborough II
Fleetwood
Folkestone II
Folkestone III
The Forest of Dean Revisited
Frome
Fulham

Galashiels
Around Gillingham
Gloucestershire at Work
North Gloucestershire at
    War
South Gloucestershire at War
Goudhurst to Tenterden
Grantham
Great Yarmouth II
Greenwich
Greenwich & Woolwich

Hackney II
Hackney, Homerton & Dalston
From Haldon to Mid-
    Dartmoor
Hammersmith & Shepherd's
    Bush
Hampstead to Primrose Hill
Around Harrogate
Harrow & Pinner
Hastings & St Leonards
Hayes & West Drayton
Around Haywards Heath
Around Helston
Around Henley-on-Thames
Herefordshire
Around Highworth
Hitchin
Holderness
Hong Kong
Huddersfield II
Huddersfield III

Ilford to Hainault
Ilfracombe
Ipswich Revisited

Islington
Jersey III

Kendal Revisited
Kensington & Chelsea
East Kent at War
Keswick & the Central Lakes
Kingston
Kirkby & District
Kirkby & District II
Kirkby Lonsdale
Knowle & Dorridge

The Lake Counties at Work
Lambeth, Kennington &
    Clapham
Lancashire
The Lancashire Coast
Lancashire Railways
East Lancashire at War
Lancing & Sompting
Leeds in the News
Around Leek
East of Leicester
Leicester at Work
Leicestershire People
Letchworth
Lewisham & Deptford III
Lincoln
Lincoln Cathedral
The Lincolnshire Coast
The Lincolnshire Wolds
Liverpool
Llandudno
Around Lochaber
Theatrical London
Loughborough
Lowestoft
Luton
Lye & Wollescote
Lympne Airfield
Lytham St Annes

Around Maidenhead
Manchester
Manchester Road & Rail
Mansfield

Margate II
Marlborough II
Marylebone & PaddingtonThe
  Melton Mowbray Album
The History of the Melton
  Mowbray Pork Pie
Merton, Morden & Mitcham
Middlesbrough
Around Mildenhall
Milton Keynes
Minehead

The Nadder Valley
Newark
The Norfolk Broads
Norfolk at Work
North Walsham & District
Northallerton
Around Norwich
Nottingham Yesterday
  & Today

Oldham
Ormskirk & District
Otley & District
Oxford Yesterday & Today
Oxfordshire at Play
Oxfordshire at School
Oxfordshire Yesterday & Today

Penwith
Penzance & Newlyn
Around Pershore
Peterborough
Around Plymouth
Poole
Portslade

Prestwich
Putney & Roehampton

Redditch & the Needle
  District
Richmond
Rickmansworth
The River Soar
Around Rotherham
Royal Norfolk Regiment
Rugby & District II
Ruislip
Around Rutland
Around Ryde

Saffron Walden
St Albans
St Andrews
Salford
Salisbury II
Sandhurst & Crowthorne
Sandown & Shanklin
Around Seaton & Sidmouth
Sedgley & District
Sedgley & District II
Sheffield
Sherwood Forest
Shoreham-by-Sea
Lost Shrewsbury
Southampton
Southend-on-Sea
Southwark, Bermondsey &
  Rotherhithe
Southwark, Bermondsey &
  Rotherhithe II
Southwell
Stafford

Around Staveley
Stepney, Bethnal Green &
  Poplar
The History of Stilton
  Cheese
Stockport
Stoke Newington, Stamford
  Hill & Upper Clapton
Stourbridge, Wollaston &
  Amblecote
Stowmarket
Stratford, West Ham & the
  Royal Docks
Streatham II
Stretford
Stroud & the Five Valleys
Stroud & the Five Valleys II
Suffolk
Suffolk at Work II
Sunderland
Sutton
A Swindon Album
Swindon III

Around Tamworth
Along the Thames
Around Thirsk
Tipton
Tipton II
Around Tonbridge
Torquay
Around Truro
Twickenham, Hampton &
  Teddington

Uley, Dursley & Cam
Upminster & Hornchurch

The Upper Fal
Uxbridge 1950–1970

Ventnor

Wallingford
Walsall Revisited
Waltham Abbey
Walton-on-Thames &
  Weybridge
Wandsworth at War
Around Warwick
Weardale
Weardale II
Wednesbury
Wembley & Kingsbury
West Wight
Weymouth & Portland
Around Wheatley
Around Whetstone,
  Totteridge & Finchley
Whitchurch to Market
  Drayton
Wigton & the Solway
  Plain
Willesden
Wimbledon
Around Windsor
Wisbech
Witham & District
The Witney District
Wokingham
The Women's Land Army
Woolwich
Worcestershire at Work
Wordsworth's Lakeland
Wotton-under-Edge to
  Chipping Sodbury

SUTTON'S PHOTOGRAPHIC HISTORY OF TRANSPORT

Jaguar
Jensen & Jensen-Healey
Lotus
Morgan
Rolls-Royce

TVR
Vauxhall
Suffolk Transport
Manchester Road & Rail
Manchester Ship Canal

Black Country Railways
Cheshire Railways
Derbyshire Railways
Devon Railways
Lancashire Railways

Shropshire Railways
Warwickshire Railways
Worcestershire Railways
Steam around Reading
Steam around Salisbury

To order any of these titles please telephone our distributor, Littlehampton Book Services on 01903 828800
For a catalogue of these and our other titles please ring Emma Leitch on 01453 731114